# The Other Alberta:

## Decoding a Political Enigma

*To my husband, Derek Brown, my son, Michael and all those who have made this book possible*

# The Other Alberta:

## Decoding a Political Enigma

*Doreen Barrie*

To, Donna,
Fighting for the Other Alberta!
Doreen

2006

UNIVERSITY OF
REGINA

CANADIAN PLAINS
RESEARCH CENTER

Canadian Plains Research Center
University of Regina
Regina, Saskatchewan S4S 0A2
Canada
Tel: (306) 585-4758
Fax: (306) 585-4699
e-mail: canadian.plains@uregina.ca
http://www.cprc.uregina.ca

**Library and Archives Canada Cataloguing in Publication**
Barrie, Doreen Patricia
The other Alberta : decoding a political enigma / Doreen Barrie.

(Trade books based in scholarship ; 16)
Includes bibliographical references and index.
ISBN 0-88977-192-8

1. Alberta—Politics and government—1905–. 2. Alberta—History—1905–.
I. University of Regina. Canadian Plains Research Center. II. Title. III. Series: TBS ; 16

FC3661.B37 2006          971.23
C2006-900238-X

We acknowledge the financial support of the Government of Canada through the Book Publishing Industry Development Program (BPDIP) for our publishing activities.

Cover design: Brian Danchuk Design, Regina, Saskatchewan
Index: Patricia Furdek (www.userfriendlyindexes.com)

# Contents

# Milestones and Memorable Moments

1905                        Alberta achieves provincehood

## Governments

Liberals

| | |
|---|---|
| 1905–1910 | Alexander Rutherford, Premier |
| 1910–1917 | Arthur Sifton, Premier |
| 1917–1921 | Charles Stewart, Premier |

United Farmers of Alberta (UFA)

| | |
|---|---|
| 1921–1925 | Herbert Greenfield, Premier |
| 1925–1934 | John Brownlee, Premier |
| 1934–1935 | Richard Reid, Premier |

Social Credit

| | |
|---|---|
| 1935–1943 | William Aberhart, Premier |
| 1943–1968 | Ernest Manning, Premier |
| 1968–1971 | Harry Strom, Premier |

Progressive Conservatives (PC)

| | |
|---|---|
| 1971–1985 | Peter Lougheed |
| 1985–1992 | Don Getty, Premier |
| 1992–present | Ralph Klein, Premier |

## Other Notable Events

| | |
|---|---|
| 1917 | First woman in the British Empire, Louise McKinney, takes her seat in the Alberta legislature |
| March 1919 | Meeting in Calgary to organize One Big Union |
| May 1919 | Winnipeg General Strike begins |
| 1923 | Alberta Wheat Pool established |
| 1930 | Prairie provinces obtain ownership of their land and natural resources |
| February 1947 | Oil strike at Leduc transforms Alberta's economy |
| October 1973 | Oil prices quadruple as the Organization of Petroleum Exporting Countries impose an embargo on exports to some countries |
| October 1980 | National Energy Program unveiled |
| April 1982 | Constitution Act 1982 which includes and amending formula and the Charter of Rights and Freedoms, signed by Queen Elizabeth |

# Preface

Centennial celebrations provided Albertans with an opportunity to look back at their achievements and to contemplate the legacy that will be left to future generations. At the time of writing, it is as if the economy is on steroids, benefiting mightily from soaring oil and gas prices. However as provincial coffers overflow, there is an undertow of anxiety that a bust must inevitably follow.

Volatile commodity prices are familiar to Albertans, so fears of a collapse are not unfounded. Media reports of resentment and envy in other provinces fuel the suspicion that this is a rerun of an old movie and some of the province's wealth will be skimmed off by Ottawa. As the debate over Alberta's affluence rages, it is entirely possible that the rest of Canada will get the impression that as *nouveau riche* Albertans gloat over their good fortune, they care little about the rest of the country. Nothing could be further from the truth, but as there is some hysteria about a possible raid on the treasury, mixed signals are emanating from the province. Albertans have a tendency to swagger a bit, to delight in their good fortune, but I do not believe we are mean-spirited.

This book is intended to rectify some misconceptions about this province. It covers a lot of ground as the Alberta story can only be understood against the backdrop of earlier events. In our current affluent circumstances it is useful to be reminded that Alberta's pioneers were less fortunate. They had to cope with poverty, foreclosures and crop failures. As they struggled to come to terms with their circumstances, their mettle was tested and their legacy shows they were up to the challenge.

At the outset, I had a very different book in mind but part way through I decided to target a wider audience. Consequently, I have tried to write in an accessible style with a degree of informality (and a few feeble attempts at humour) that is not characteristic of academic writing. However, I will not insult my audience by dumbing down the material. I have cited references so readers can check the accuracy of quotes because much of what I have written rests on analyses done by others.

This book is a product of the 15 years I have taught Alberta politics and the many more years I have studied it. As I have spent most of my life here, the analysis is based, in part, on observations and insights I have gained from students, from being active in the community, and having a husband and family members in the oil patch. All these contribute to the wide sweep of the analysis. I hope it will help Albertans understand themselves and will contribute to a better understanding of Alberta outside the province. My views are bound to provoke discussion but I hope they will also result in some soul searching.

Doreen Barrie
Calgary, Alberta

Postscript: As this book goes to press, a new Conservative Prime Minister has been sworn-in. Having achieved the long-awaited prize of national office, the Party's Reform/Alliance wing is buoyed by high expectations. As longtime supporters of the Party, they expect to be repaid for their loyalty and to play a key role in the new administration. However, there are already murmurings that the Progressive Conservative element is having too much influence on Stephen Harper.

The Prime Minister has an unenviable task as he performs a delicate balancing act: shoring up his Alberta base while convincing voters in Central Canada that the Conservatives are a truly national party. This requires wooing voters primarily in Ontario and Quebec, which might be interpreted as a betrayal by some loyalists. If the new Party seems to be turning its back on its origins and behaving just like the parties it has replaced, it is entirely possible that a disgruntled rump will drift away and form yet another protest party in the future.

# Introduction

Alberta entered its second century as an attractive destination for migrants from other parts of the country as well as immigrants from around the world. Affluence has not been the norm; the last hundred years of provincehood have brought prosperity and despair in equal measure. The boom and bust nature of the economy results in a degree of volatility unmatched in any other jurisdiction in North America. While the discovery of oil produced wealth it did not provide economic stability, nor has it conferred political clout. Albertans are often frustrated at their lack of political influence, and as they cry all the way to the bank, Canadians elsewhere are mystified.

The province is an enigma to many and it would not be an exaggeration to say that, with the exception of Quebec, no other province is less understood. Misconceptions about Alberta abound within the province as well as outside. In other words, the perception Albertans have of themselves is as questionable as the view the rest of the country has of Albertans. For this reason, I felt that the post-centennial would be an appropriate moment to question the conventional wisdom about Alberta and to shed some light on another Alberta, one that exists in spaces that slip through large media filters. Mark Lisac has recently undertaken a similar exercise, so I am not alone in wanting to look at this province through a different prism (Lisac, 2004).[1] This analysis will certainly be controversial, but I hope it will provide a more textured and nuanced look at a province that often attracts attention for the wrong reasons.

There are good reasons for believing that Alberta is a province *pas comme les autres*. It stepped out of the political mainstream for half a century, voting for home-grown parties and this "fall from grace" is believed to have left an indelible mark. Even though it has returned to the traditional party fold, it does not seem to fit the traditional party mould. Add the fact that Alberta's history is punctuated with a cast of colourful characters, political innovation and controversial monetary theories, and the stage is set to view its inhabitants as a breed apart. There have been heroes and villains aplenty, protest parties and perennial dissatisfaction with the status quo—all of which have provided entertainment and sometimes provoked derision outside the province.

It would be fair to say that the stereotypical image of Alberta is that of a parochial province peopled with right-wing rednecks who wear cowboy boots and hold attitudes to match. Ironically, the cowboy image is carefully cultivated and celebrated every year at the Calgary Stampede when the entire city is transformed into a Wild West theme park. For about ten days every July, people who would not know the difference between a branding iron and a curling iron, dress "Western" for the duration of the Stampede. Few workplaces are immune to Stampede fever and demand for straw bales and rope soars as they compete to present the most authentic western motif. For the rest of the year, some components of the western heritage are embraced enthusiastically, but the negative connotations of "cowboy" are rejected by Calgarians. An interesting sidebar is that the Calgary Stampede has branded the entire province with the cowboy image.[2]

There are other facets to Alberta that are seldom remembered, aspects which present a very different picture of the province. It is here that in 1917 the first women, Louise McKinney and Lt. Roberta

---

1. In order to avoid cluttering up the text with footnotes, references will be keyed to a bibliography at the end. The author's name, the year of publication and the page number will appear in parentheses for each citation. The notation "n.d." means that there was no date on the source.

2. Edmonton has a rival festival, Klondike Days, which is less well-known but its Fringe Festival is famous.

McAdams, were elected to a legislature in the British Empire.[3] McKinney is better known as one of the "Famous Five" Alberta women who launched the "Persons case." At issue in this case was whether women should be regarded as "persons" and, therefore, eligible to be appointed to the Senate.[4] Another trail blazer was Irene Parlby, a member of the United Farmers of Alberta government who was appointed to Cabinet in 1921. She was the first female Cabinet minister in the British Empire. Nellie McClung was also a member of the 1921 legislature but she was elected as a Liberal. Ernest Manning, at 27, was the youngest-ever Cabinet minister in the Commonwealth. In conjunction with the other prairie provinces, Alberta has effected a permanent transformation of the Canadian political landscape but these achievements have, for the most part, been lost in the mists of history.

The progressive (this depends on one's point of view) aspect of Alberta has been buried, and the excitement and turmoil that gripped the province for decades has been overlaid by a layer of conservatism. Even a brief examination of the province's early history reveals that there were other strands in the ideological tapestry that seems mono-chromatic today.

During World War I, farmers across the country endorsed the Farmers' Platform which listed demands from the agricultural communi-ty. The Platform, which was widely supported in Alberta, had a strong socialist flavour. So did the Non-Partisan League which elected two members to the legislature in 1917. Another indicator that Albertans were not hesitant to challenge the status quo was the radical One Big Union (OBU) which was formed in Calgary in 1919. Founders of the OBU expressed admiration for the Soviet system of government and talked of overthrowing the capitalist system. The Co-operative Commonwealth Federation (CCF), precursor to the New Democratic Party, had its founding convention in Calgary in 1932. Communists

---

3. McAdams was elected by the armed forces overseas so she was not in the legislature on the day it opened. Thus she was not sworn in with McKinney who became the first woman to be sworn in and take her seat in a legislature in the British Empire (Elections Canada, 2001: 25).

4. Women were recognized as legal "persons" in Alberta in 1917, the first jurisdiction in Canada to do so.

were elected as municipal councillors and were active in helping the destitute during the Depression. The truth is that Alberta had a turbulent early history as it came to terms with being an unimportant peripheral province in the Canadian Confederation. If Albertans had been "in on the creation" of Canada, they would have rewritten the script.

It is curious that we know so little of the early radical tendencies and one may well ask if they have been completely obliterated. In the postwar period, the discovery of oil and the affluence that it heralded muted the early radicalism. In addition, certain historical events have been edited from Alberta's history since the 1940s, by political and social elites. Since then a new identity has been created using a different set of raw materials. It was mainly after Ernest Manning took over the reins of the Social Credit Party that the outlines of this new image began to emerge. Initially, it was a tactical move to address the threat of the CCF during the 1944 election but as the province became more affluent, the turn to the right became a permanent feature of Social Credit's policy platform. This new image emphasized innovation, self-reliance and a willingness to take risks. This "official" version of what constitutes an Albertan (a version adopted by the Conservatives when they came to power) is questionable, reading like a promotional brochure which glosses over inconvenient facts and focuses on selective elements.

That many people are confused about conflicting images of Albertans is not surprising: which perception is false, the negative image of the redneck or the more positive one of the rugged individualist of modern Alberta folklore? Is Alberta a distinct society? In some ways it is, but there is ample evidence that Albertans resemble their counterparts in other provinces in fundamental ways. As a large proportion of the population (approximately 43% according to the 2001 census) is from elsewhere, one would have to believe that something in the air and the water transforms newcomers into instant Albertans!

This is not to suggest that Albertans are identical to other Canadians or that there are no differences among the provinces. What will become apparent in the discussion to follow, is that people are shaped by their shared histories and experiences and as provincial boundaries ensure different sets of experiences, each province will have a unique character. What is different about Alberta is that, for most of its history, opposition has been fragmented, giving governing parties a clear field. Although voters were not of one mind, as opposition did not have a single partisan vehicle to sustain it, dissent was splintered and muted. As a result, the government of the day is assumed to be the Voice of Alberta, speaking for a united, homogeneous population.

In his book *The Klein Revolution*, Mark Lisac points out that this is an artificial homogeneity as it portrays a population that is unidimensional (1995: 145). Governments in the province have been successful in deflecting attention towards the deficiencies of the federal government and away from any shortcomings of the provincial government. In these contemporary intergovernmental battles, the population invariably lines up behind the Premier like Albertans did generations ago. Ralph Klein has criticized Ottawa's foreign policy stance on Iraq, threatened to violate the Canada Health Act and opposes the Kyoto Accord. These are but a few recent examples of the continuing campaign against the federal government, a campaign to make Ottawa the *de facto* opposition party in Alberta. In the pages that follow, we will explore the way in which a unique Alberta identity has been forged in part by driving a wedge between Albertans and the national government and, by extension, the national community.

This book is intended to have general appeal, primarily to Albertans curious to know what makes us tick, but it may interest Canadians in other provinces who are baffled by Alberta. The reader will be acquainted with events in the province's history which have contributed to an ongoing scepticism about political parties, particularly "old line" political parties and the legitimacy of opposition. Early experiences have caused Albertans to adopt a very protective attitude towards natural resources and we will examine how decisions made a century ago cast a long shadow. The salience of natural resource ownership is underlined in the comments made by Peter Lougheed in a speech marking Alberta's 75th anniversary. The Premier remarked that in 1930:

> a celebration occurred in Alberta almost equal to (and some say stronger than) that of 1905 in intensity and feeling, with the passage of the Natural Resources Transfer Act. It was deemed by the then-premier as the most important piece of legislation that would ever come before the Legislative Assembly. To this day most Albertans concur with that judgement (quoted in Pratt, 1981: 164).

Gaining ownership of resources marked a coming of age for the province, and in Alberta's centennial year resources were once again in the spotlight.

Being the "Last Best West," the last destination in North America to attract large waves of immigrants, had consequences which produced an appetite for home-grown banks and a distrust of Eastern financial institutions. Distrust of banks ensured Albertans were more receptive to the Social Credit Party's critique of the financial system. The link between these defining moments and Alberta's political culture will be drawn to demonstrate how they influence contemporary issues and attitudes. The province's early history provides the raw materials which animate politics in the 21st century and we will see how selective elements are utilized to muster support to this day.

Citations will be used sparingly, but some are essential. It will also be necessary to explain some political science concepts like political culture and the role played by narratives, myths and symbols.

Although the book is primarily about Alberta, it may be of more general interest as it examines how an identity can be constructed and public opinion sculpted. In any democratic country, policies must be sold to voters and these are sometimes highly controversial. The way in which populations are mobilized presents some fascinating insights into our capacity to be manipulated.

By the end of the book readers should be able to decide whether Albertans are indeed a breed apart, very different from people in other provinces. In addition they will be able to identify the sophisticated techniques used in the contemporary era to influence the way in which citizens see their political world.

# 1

# A Province is Born

As newly minted Albertans marched in an inaugural parade on September 1, 1905 they could never have imagined what the province would be like a century later. Who could have dreamt that the family farm would be an endangered species, that oil and gas would make us fabulously wealthy or that the province, prior to its centennial, would punch above its political weight. From being citizens of a federal territory, they were now Albertans and had to define themselves as they negotiated their new status. Many challenges awaited citizens of this brand new province and they dealt with them in innovative ways which altered the political landscape. There was frustration surrounding the region's role in Confederation and some of the early experiences embittered Albertans. We will look at the pivotal events that occurred in the province's first decade and explore the profound influence they have had on the way citizens of the infant province would see themselves and their place in the larger Canadian community. The infant turned out to be rather colicky!

## Formative Events
New political entities do not emerge fully formed at the moment of their birth, but neither are they blank canvases awaiting strokes from a brush. Thus, some of the raw materials of the new Alberta identity existed prior

to the attainment of provincehood. In the late 1880s there were battles between the Territorial Legislature and the federal government as representatives fought to wrest greater control over revenue from the appointed executive. Subsequently, there was pressure on Ottawa to grant provincial status. The campaign was spearheaded by Frederick Haultain, "an English-born, Ontario-raised, but Alberta-spirited lawyer" who was Premier of the North-West Territories (van Herk, 2001: 206). Haultain was not enamoured of partisanship in the legislature and signalled his disdain for it by appointing Liberals as well as Conservatives to his Cabinet. His views on this matter are summed up in a farewell speech he made to his constituents in Fort Macleod:

> As for myself, I stand for no-party government, regardless of what any political party or both political parties may decide. The welfare and interests of this great western country are more important than the success or convenience of any political party (quoted in Pal, 1992: 7).

These sentiments were reinforced during the term of Alberta's first administration under Premier Alexander Rutherford.

A preference for non-partisanship became a key component of the distinctive Alberta mindset alongside the popularity of the mechanisms of direct democracy and a protective attitude towards natural resources. The latter has contributed to the way in which federal-provincial interaction takes place and the way Albertans respond to this relationship. As we shall see, there is a combative attitude towards Ottawa and a sort of quiescence in relation to the provincial government. In those early years Albertans confronted situations which left an indelible mark on them, a mark that might have faded had it not been reinforced by later events and later governments. Consequently, they continue to animate political discourse in contemporary Alberta.

The set of attitudes (towards non-partisanship, direct democracy and natural resource ownership) provides a continuing theme running through the province's history and provides the building blocks of its political culture. To a lesser extent, Albertans were shaped by their experiences with banks and debt. Debt was particularly onerous because Alberta was the last agricultural frontier on the continent and money was expensive when farmers had to borrow. The fact that Alberta defaulted on its loans during the Depression is also a shameful memory.

Beginning in 1905 the Alberta government was preoccupied with building a legislature, setting up the judicial system and other ingredients of a political system. Waves of immigrants were flocking to the province, so such practical matters preoccupied the government of the day.[1] Alberta's first government was Liberal, as was every government until 1921. Electoral success over a decade and a half, however, masked the growing dissatisfaction of the population with the provincial Liberals in particular, and party politics more generally. The region's marginal role and lack of influence at the centre was demonstrated very early and the legacy is at best a wariness, and at worst deep suspicion about major national initiatives. To this day they are assessed through the lens of regional interest.

## The Roots of Non-partisanship

As mentioned earlier, the seeds of non-partisanship were sown by Haultain prior to the attainment of provincehood. When Alberta and Saskatchewan were territories of the federal government the role of the legislature was mainly administration of the territory. The relationship between Ottawa and the North-West Territories was colonial, not unlike that between Canada and Britain prior to Confederation. The degree of political autonomy was very circumscribed and the territorial govern-ment was primarily concerned with petitioning the federal government for things such as schools, roads and bridges. As a result, partisanship in the Territorial Legislature was largely irrelevant because the two parties were in agreement about what was required by settlers who had already begun to flow into the province. This view on partisanship might not have survived in the new province if events had not breathed new life into it.

In the 1909 election campaign Cornelius Hiebert, one of two Conservative members in the first legislature, left the party and ran as an Independent, arguing that he wanted the freedom to speak his own mind. He contended that "the bitter enmities of party strife have no place in provincial affairs" (Thomas, 1959: 68). What prompted Hiebert to echo the sentiments expressed by Haultain?

---

1. The population increased more than five-fold between 1901 and 1911—i.e. just before and after provincehood was attained. From a mere 73,000 at the turn of the century, the population leapt to 374,000 in 1911 (Palmer and Palmer, 1990: 14).

Negative views of partisan politics were connected with attitudes towards political parties—parties that were considered "foreign" to prairie soil. In more settled parts of Canada, political institutions inherited from Britain evolved and adapted to Canadian conditions over a long period of time. On the Prairies this process was accelerated so when parties and political practices "imported" from eastern Canada appeared to work against the region's interest, they gave rise to resentment and ultimately, outright rejection.

The problem was that the script called for the Prairies to be a hinterland growing crops for export and providing a captive market for manufactured goods produced in Central Canada. The National Policy, implemented long before Alberta was a twinkle in Ottawa's eye, set up tariffs that forced the farming community to buy Canadian-made farm equipment (as well as everything else) that they could have bought more cheaply just across the border. It did not help that their wheat was sold on an unprotected international market. The prairie provinces were, in a sense, "Children of Confederation," and residents resented the inferior role they were intended to play. There was a consensus on the causes of the problems so they saw no need for partisan debate. To compound the problem, elected officials, whether federal or provincial, could do little to change the situation or the policies put in place decades ago to tie the country together, however imperfectly, from east to west.

The preference for non-partisanship made some sense in a territory administered from Ottawa and its popularity should have declined given the passage of time, as it did in Saskatchewan and Manitoba. However, an early, bitter experience led to disillusionment with parties, especially eastern-based parties, and the party system itself.

The first nail in the coffin of political parties, the one that Thomas describes as the "pivotal fact in Alberta politics" was the Alberta & Great Waterways Railway (A&GW) crisis. This shook party organizations and the public conscience and nudged political behaviour away from the conventional path (1959: 93).[2]

As this scandal has had such serious consequences, it is important to

---

2. Information that follows was obtained from Chapters IV and V, "Alberta and the Waterways Railway, 1909–1910," and "The Sifton Government and the Railway Problem, 1910–13" (Thomas, 1959: 95–153).

## Railway Fever

*The province was in the grip of railway fever in the first decade of the century as settlers were pouring in and a network of rail lines had to be built to tie communities together. Railways were the mega-projects of Canada's first half century. In addition to the Canadian Pacific Railway (CPR), there was the Grand Trunk Pacific, Canadian Northern, the Alberta Central Railway and others. One such company, the Alberta & Great Waterways Railway (A&GW) was to construct a line from Edmonton to Fort McMurray via Lac La Biche. The latter was touted as a second Lake Louise which would attract tourists from as far away as New Orleans.*

*The Alberta government guaranteed bonds of the A&GW at preferential rates, a fact that led to allegations of wrong-doing on the part of some government members. The scandal dominated the last legislative session before the 1909 election, the election itself and a large part of the Second Legislative Assembly. In a nutshell, there were accusations of corruption in high places: It was alleged that at least one cabinet minister had been bought with equity in the company and perhaps half a dozen Liberal MLAs had a financial interest in it. In an astonishing display of trust, the government had pledged the credit of the province to the tune of $7.4 million, knowing neither the directors of the company nor the extent of subscribed capital in the enterprise.*

*Premier Rutherford appointed a Royal Commission to ascertain whether government members or officials had any connection with the railway, but this did little to lower the temperature in the province. Amidst allegations of shredding of documents and the temporary disappearance of the President of A&GW, the premier stepped down in 1910 and was replaced by the Chief Justice of the province, Arthur Sifton.*

*The report of the Royal Commission concluded that neither the premier nor Attorney-General Cross, the cabinet minister involved, had any personal interest in the company. Nevertheless, the report was critical of both men for placing the province in a position of potential liability on the basis of information that was misleading, unreliable and in some cases, absolutely false (Thomas, 1959: 95–153).*

understand the most important details which are summarized in the box on the preceding page ("Railway Fever"). It is the fallout from the scandal that is our concern. By far the most crucial aspect of this scandal is that it reverberated through the province for several years, subjecting the Liberal Party and the opposition Conservatives to a degree of scrutiny at a critical juncture in Alberta's history. The parties were, in a sense, on probation during that time and their performance was found wanting. As this incident had such far-reaching implications, it is worth examining it in some detail.

The A&GW railway was just one part of the network being built in the province. The new Premier Alexander Rutherford had ambitious plans for railways to tie different areas of the province together. He decided that if the federal government would not, the Alberta government "would guarantee the bonds of any railway that would raise 35 percent of the capital cost of its own construction" (van Herk, 2001: 225). This was a disastrous mistake.

The Liberal government's conduct on this issue did not endear the administration to Albertans. However, the Liberal stumble did not benefit the opposition Conservative Party for two reasons: first it was government backbenchers, not the opposition, who first raised the matter in the legislature and thus brought it to public notice. If anything, this probably reinforced non-partisan attitudes by underlining the fact that opposition was redundant. The second reason why the Conservatives could not capitalize on the Liberals' problems was that their leader, R.B. Bennett, was the solicitor for the unpopular CPR. The corporation was regarded by the farming community as an exploitative instrument of Eastern Canadian interests (Barr, 1971: 12), so Bennett's connection with the railway tarnished his credibility.

Money from the sale of bonds to finance the railway had been lodged with several banks in the province. As A&GW had failed to live up to its commitments, the provincial government attempted to recover the bond money. The banks refused to release it to the provincial treasurer and so began a protracted legal battle on this dispute. This was an event that Albertans had cause to remember later when they had bitter experiences with financial institutions.

Bennett denounced the government's move and predicted that the action would have international repercussions which would reflect badly on the province's reputation. Albertans who watched the spectacle were concerned about the large sum ($7.4 million) of provincial money that was unavailable to the government but which was earning 5% for bond holders. While Bennett might have been defending a principle, his position seemed to be driven more by the interests of his employers than by the interests of Albertans. Thus the Conservative Party could not capitalize on the political crisis created by the railway scandal.[3]

Just as Canadians were transfixed in 2005 by the Gomery Enquiry into the sponsorship scandal, Albertans watched with great interest as events unfolded around 1910. This was an extremely unfortunate and unpleasant introduction to party politics in the province. It is hard to imagine, but the general public paid keen attention to day-to-day politics in those days. Their attention spans must have been much longer too because people in the gallery at the legislature sat spellbound when Bennett gave a five-hour speech which ended at midnight. One group that was especially vigilant was the United Farmers of Alberta (UFA). The organization had recently come into existence after the merger of two farming groups, the Canadian Society of Equity and the Alberta Farmers' Association.

As Thomas argues, the Alberta & Great Waterways fiasco left an enduring legacy in the province. Although there was no immediate rejection of the major parties, as the case with the banks dragged on for years, the shadow of the rail crisis hovered over the province until the next election. World War I intervened, postponing the impact of the scandal until 1921. However, two candidates from the Non-Partisan League won seats in the 1917 provincial election, demonstrating that non-partisanship was alive in the province.

In the 1921 election political parties were denounced, and the UFA which was swept into power claimed it was not a political party. From the turn of the century to the 1990s, this claim has echoed and re-echoed in the province as the governing party has invariably disdained "politics" and stressed that it speaks for all Albertans, delivering good government based on a provincial consensus. Pal argues that support for

---

3. The case worked its way through the judicial system up to the Judicial Committee for the Privy Council in London. At that time, this was the final court of appeal for constitutional cases in Canada. The province lost the case there.

non-partisanship is rooted in the semi-colonial situation prior to 1905 and experiences shortly thereafter. However, "once the discourse was established, it nurtured every political leader that Alberta has ever produced" (Pal, 1992: 23). Distrust of political parties led logically to the popularity of political forms which would enable voters to have greater input into the political process.

## Direct Democracy

Albertans have long been fans of direct democracy, i.e., populist measures designed to ensure voters can influence elected representatives between elections. As we shall see, despite support for these ideas, there was little concrete evidence that governing parties were equally supportive. In frontier societies the political rules of the game were a work in progress and citizens took great interest in them as the laws that were being formulated often had a direct impact on their lives. The identity of interest within the farming community meant that a sort of bush telegraph was at work which kept farmers abreast of developments. Keep in mind as well that when Alberta was being settled, there was little competition for the attention of the people from radio, television and other entertainment. Thus political discussion was the stuff of everyday conversations.

Prairie farmers were influenced by ideas that swirled around the agrarian community in the US and by the solutions that were attempted there. As early as the 1909 election campaign, the Conservatives promised to adopt initiative, referendum and recall—devices of direct democracy that were being utilized in some western states. The weapons of direct democracy worked better within the American political system where the life of a government does not depend on maintaining majority support in the legislature. As farmers made some gains there, it is not surprising that these ideas spilled over the border and were brought in by American immigrants.

The parliamentary system does not serve the small provinces well. As the principle of responsible government means the government must resign if it lacks majority support in the legislature, MPs must toe the party line.[4] This, combined with the cloak of secrecy surrounding caucus and Cabinet deliberations, means that MPs from the periphery cannot speak out against policies that have a negative impact on their regions. As far as voters are concerned, what you see is what you get: an individual whose concerns for regional interests seem to be swallowed by the black hole that is Ottawa. Little wonder then that the first genera-tion of Albertans who had little understanding of the Westminster-style parliamentary system should look south for solutions.

The influence of farmers was growing with the creation of the UFA in 1910 and one of their demands was for greater input into legislation. The government of Arthur Sifton acceded to their request, and in 1913 passed the Direct Legislation Act that permitted voters to initiate legis-lation through a petition. If the proposal received the required number of signatures, the government was obliged to hold a referendum on the peti-tion and to pass the legislation with only minor changes. The Act also gave voters the right to demand a referendum on legislation that had been passed during a session, thus giving them a sort of suspensive veto.[5]

The Act was repealed in 1959 when Ernest Manning was Premier. The legislation was a response to frustration at the apparent lack of pop-ular input into government policy. However, as the sources of agrarian frustration—freight rates, tariffs and transportation policy—were mat-ters that were within federal jurisdiction, provincial legislation could do nothing to address the main sources of farmers' dissatisfaction.

---

4. In Canada, party discipline is much more stringent than in other Westminster-style parliamentary systems. There is no reason why Canada should not follow Britain's example and allow elected members more flexibility. In the United Kingdom, MPs are not kept on such a short leash and are allowed to vote against the party under certain circumstances.

5. If the Direct Legislation Act was still in effect, a group of citizens could, for example, start a petition regarding electricity deregulation or drilling for oil and gas near major cities. Albertans used the initiative only once, in 1915, when they signed a petition for legislation on prohibition. The referendum was held, people voted in favour and the government dutifully passed the requisite legislation (Watkins, 1980: 51). Had there been a constitutional challenge, the Act may have been struck down. In 1919, Manitoba referred a similar bill to the Supreme Court which ruled it unconstitutional because it infringed on the Lieutenant-Governor's powers of reservation. This power allows the Lieutenant-Governor to "reserve" a piece of provincial legislation (in effect vetoing it by sending it to Ottawa) instead of giving it royal assent. Legislation that was a product of a citizen's initiative removed the power of the legislature to amend it and the Lieutenant-Governor's right to reserve it. Changing the Lieutenant-Governor's powers is outside provincial jurisdiction. The Alberta legislation was slightly different and might have escaped.

There was renewed interest in these populist ideas as the Reform Party, and later the Canadian Alliance, embraced them as part of their platform. What this indicates is a familiar frustration with the perceived insensitivity of the party in power to the concerns citizens have between elections. There have been periodic promises of parliamentary reform to address the issue, but so far not much has changed.

If the farming community had exploited the potential of the parliamentary system, especially in the 1920s when the Progressives, the federal wing of Farmers' Parties, held the balance of power, they might have wrung more changes out of Ottawa. Similarly, if the Canadian Senate had played its intended role as champion of small provinces, regional discontent would have been dampened. So many ifs... In the event, frustrated by their political impotence, Canadian farmers yearned for the greener political pastures enjoyed by their American counterparts.

It is worth mentioning that quite apart from the fact that populist devices are generally incompatible with the parliamentary system, populist devices can be misused. In some American states which have a provision for citizens' initiatives, the process has been distorted to such an extent that only those with financial resources can hope to succeed in initiating legislation. Powerful groups have been successful in introducing initiatives by hiring professionals to run campaigns and obtain signatures. In addition, individuals are paid to sign a petition. Thus a mechanism that was designed to give voice to the "little guy" is being used to benefit the powerful (Ellis, 2002).

Another contribution to the seed bed of ideas came from prominent individuals in the farming community such as Henry Wise Wood who was president of the UFA when it formed the government in 1921. He was not interested in political office. Wood was an American who had moved to the province after having been active in the agrarian movement in the United States. Wood and others like him came to their new home and proposed political solutions which had been tried in the US where the system was congenial to them. Thus ideas revolving around direct democracy flowed into the province both directly and indirectly.

*Natural Resource Ownership*
Another formative experience that cast a long shadow over the province was the decision by Ottawa to retain ownership of the land and

natural resources of the prairie provinces. This decision was made to ensure swift and orderly settlement in the region as there were fears that the Americans were casting covetous eyes north. Settlement of the western US was complete because by 1880 there was no free land available. As Macpherson observes:

> Unlike the provinces which had entered Confederation at the beginning, the prairie provinces were creations of the federal government and the federal government retained control over their natural resources until 1930. They were not equal members of a federation; the federal government was to them not only a federal but an imperial government. It was therefore essential to the purposes of the provincial community that its government should be an effective offensive and defensive weapon against this imperial power (1962: 21).

This fateful decision affected the relationship between Alberta and Ottawa and retains salience to this day. Macpherson contends that even after provincehood was achieved, the relationship between the federal government and the Prairies continued to be quasi-colonial and the natural resource issue gave rise to the notion that Alberta, along with Saskatchewan and Manitoba, was a second-class province. The quasi-colonial relationship fostered and reinforced the non-partisan attitude towards politics in Alberta.[6] If political battles were waged primarily between provincial governments and the federal government there would be no need for alternation of parties.

Keeping control over the land was controversial even if it could be justified on the grounds that it was necessary to populate the empty plains quickly to prevent the Americans from claiming the territory. Retaining ownership over natural resources was less contentious at the time as the provinces were oblivious to the wealth locked up beneath the soil. Even after oil and gas were discovered in Alberta, there was greater concern about the federal government's neglect of the resource

---

6. What is puzzling is why, given their similar status, Saskatchewan and Manitoba did not replicate Alberta's attitude towards opposition parties. Macpherson contends that Alberta's population was homogeneous, and as a result there were few divisions within the electorate. His analysis has been criticized on this point (Bell, 1985). Arguably, the Saskatchewan population was much more homogeneous than Alberta's, yet the non-partisan tradition had taken firm root only in the Alberta soil.

than Ottawa reaping the benefits it derived from owning them. As we shall see, ownership of natural resources remained a major issue in Alberta because of the oil and gas industry. As the bulk of Alberta's petroleum resources are exported outside the province, the federal government has a role to play. The way it has chosen to play this role has been a bone of contention for many Albertans.

## Suspicion of Banks
This issue has less significance than the others, but the first brush with financial institutions came when the province was attempting to get access to bond money that was lodged with them during the railway scandal. Although the refusal to release the money to the provincial government did not affect Albertans (except to the extent that it was taxpayers' money), they did take note. Later on, they did have bitter experiences which triggered demands for a moratorium on debt. The Alberta Treasury Branches (now known as ATB Financial) are a legacy of the negative attitude towards eastern-based financial institutions.

These building blocks—lingering suspicion of partisan politics, an enduring faith in consensus politics (i.e. a non-partisan approach to addressing major policy issues)—combined with residual scepticism of Ottawa's intentions regarding Alberta's resources, find contemporary expression in the generally positive attitudes towards Alberta politicians and government policies. These are unique to Alberta's political culture, and when we follow the strands of these early experiences it will become obvious why they have persisted.

Throughout our lives we encounter many things which fade from our memories over the course of time. On the other hand, some leave a mark that can never be erased. The formative events in Alberta's history which we have been discussing fall into the latter category because they have been reinforced by successive governments and Premiers. The process of reinforcement is our next focus.

# 2

# Solidifying the Memories

As any student of history knows, there is no one true version either of current events or what took place in the past. There are conflicting accounts because different historians can interpret the same set of events in different ways. History, then, is telling a story, constructing a narrative, but telling it in a way that emphasizes certain elements and glosses over or omits others. For example, feminists have noted the virtual absence of women in history books (labelling it "his-story") and are seeking to uncover the role women have played in numerous contexts from the opening up of the West to the birth of the welfare state. Some things are lost on the cutting floor of history-making while others are elevated to positions of great prominence. It is in the process of socialization that individuals learn the importance of certain memories and when recollections fade it is the historical record that keeps the collective memory alive.

There is a great deal of research on the development of collective memories and identities. One researcher, Margaret Conrad (2001), referring to the regional aspect of memories, states that they "often serve as a source of inspiration, motivation and even culprits." Conrad's research focused on Atlantic Canada but could just as easily be applied to Alberta. A similar point is made by Anthony Smith who argues that identities "are forged out of shared experiences, memories and myths, in relation to those of other collective identities," even in opposition to the identity of others (1992: 75). The Alberta case demonstrates how early disillusionment soured the first generation of citizens against political parties, the federal government and Central Canada (Alberta's "others" and "culprits") and deposited on the Alberta psyche, the first layer of dissatisfaction with the province's place in the scheme of things. Ever since, to varying degrees, these have been the oppositional "other." Founding moments in the province's history provide a glimmering of what would continue to animate politics in the future. However, their impact was not immediate.

The outbreak of World War I overshadowed all other issues in the country for a few years. During the war, while the farming community benefitted from high agricultural prices, a shortage of manpower on farms and in schools caused hardship in rural areas. Prohibition, votes for women and conscription preoccupied Albertans. Although other matters receded into the background, as subsequent events showed, the war simply postponed the political turbulence that was to shake the foundations of the party system. The consequences for traditional political parties in Alberta would be disastrous and it would be several decades before they would recover. Waiting in the wings was the UFA, which had become extremely influential with the provincial government. Legislation favourable to farmers owed its inspiration to the UFA and in fact some was virtually dictated by that group (Thomas, 1959: 166). Not surprisingly, despite calls for direct political action, Henry Wise Wood, president of the UFA from 1916, resisted, preferring to maintain the UFA as a powerful lobby group.

## Reinforcing Populist Impulses: Non-partisanship and Direct Democracy

Populist ideas struck a chord on the Prairies as farmers struggled to make their voices heard. Agrarian radicalism crossed the 49th parallel and farmers on both sides of the border expressed their dissatisfaction with a distant and indifferent federal government. Not content to cast a ballot once every four years, they sought greater consultation. Representative democracy was judged inferior to direct democracy which provided opportunities for much more participation. The farming community experimented politically via "third" parties as they experimented economically with wheat and dairy pools and co-ops. Political and economic experimentation were both attempts to gain more control over their lives. As we shall see later, the populist flame did not burn as brightly as many believe.

## The UFA

When Wood turned a deaf ear to their pleas for the UFA to enter the political arena, the farming community worked with other groups to articulate their views and to try to solve their problems. One such group was the Non-Partisan League (NPL) which had been successful in North Dakota's state elections. The NPL, which advocated a socialist platform, began to organize in Alberta in 1916 and it challenged Wood's stance on direct political action by farmers. As mentioned in the previous chapter, NPL candidates won two seats in southern Alberta in the 1917 provincial election. Following their victory, the UFA realized that the farming community was restless. Unable to contain the farmers' determination to enter the political arena, Wood capitulated but insisted that they do so as an occupational group rather than as an orthodox political party. The NPL was absorbed by the UFA.

The UFA president had definite views on how government should be conducted and the UFA's philosophy going into the 1921 election, and shortly thereafter, reflected his viewpoint. Wood was a harsh critic of political parties and "partyism" which he saw as a device to divide the community against itself. He believed that government should be conducted by occupational groups which discussed matters courteously in the legislature and reached compromises. He did not see any value in having an opposition party which adopted a contrary position merely because that was expected of opposition members. These views also expressed another recurring theme, namely that government policy should be the product of reasonable discussion rather than the cut and thrust of rowdy political battles. Farmers could relate these ideas to their own experiences: all they needed was good, common-sense advice rather than contradictory viewpoints. Thus, they were receptive to the proposition that governing did not need political parties; it consisted

## What Makes the Wild West Wild

SOURCE: GLENBOW ARCHIVES NA 3170-1

*Cartoon featured on the front of* The UFA *(the official magazine of the United Farmers of Alberta), illustrating the frustrations of the agricultural west with policies of the industrial east.*

primarily of sound administration with a dose of cooperation and compromise. Politics just muddied the waters.

The 1921 election saw the Liberals reduced to 15 seats while the leaderless UFA captured 38 and thus formed the government. Herbert Greenfield, a farmer, became the Premier. It would be an understatement to say that the UFA was surprised by the result, but the Farmers' party would not be the last to send shockwaves through the political system.

Although Wood did not choose to become Premier, his reputation in the farming community was such that his word carried great weight. He continued to serve as president of the UFA and, when the wheat pools were organized, headed the Alberta Wheat Pool. So influential was he that his biographer refers to him as the "uncrowned King of Alberta" (Rolph, 1950: 192). Wood's disdain for party politics was well known; his abhorrence of party competition was articulated repeatedly and was readily absorbed by his followers.[1] The artificial divisions encouraged by political parties were denounced by the non-partisan camp. Now the UFA's victory provided the first opportunity for a home-grown party to operate unlike the "eastern imports," especially with respect to party discipline.

The attitude of the Farmers to direct democracy can be seen in the way in which government MLAs related to their constituents. True to the belief that the interests and demands of their constituents were paramount, government MLAs did not submit to party discipline. Instead, they canvassed the views of their constituents and voted according to their wishes. This was "delegate democracy," which meant that the elected member was merely an instructed delegate who had to do the bidding of those who voted for him (or her, because by then Alberta had female MLAs). Such was the political naiveté of the UFA that they did not understand that if the government lost a major vote in the legislature, it had to resign. After a few close calls, the notion of delegate democracy was quietly dropped.

The experiment in delegate democracy was a failure at the provincial level as well as at the federal level and eventually led to the demise of the Progressives. The Progressives, the farmers' window in Ottawa, won 65 seats in the House of Commons in the 1921 election, forever breaking the two-party mould. They could have formed the Official Opposition (the Conservatives had only 50 seats) and could have played a decisive role in Mackenzie King's minority government. However, they refused to operate as a cohesive group—they did not consider themselves a political party, and they too intended to follow the wishes of their constituents. Wood conducted a running battle with Progressive leader T.A. Crerar (from Manitoba) over the role of MPs, insisting

---

1. Wood's experiences in his native country had not prepared him to operate within the parliamentary system. He had a poor understanding of the way in which the political system worked in Canada.

Alberta Members would not submit to party discipline to the detriment of their constituents' interests.[2] He also insisted that Alberta Progressives were answerable to the UFA rather than to local constituency organizations (Rolph, 1950: 118). This is an interesting twist on delegate democracy; Alberta MPs, instead of deferring to their constituents, would get their marching orders from the provincial party which also formed the provincial government. The Alberta wing presented a solid front, remaining faithful to their "uncrowned king" and his view of the world. Here we see an early example of the assumption that where federal politics are concerned, the provincial government would express the general will.

Despite Wood's vision of the provincial legislature operating on the basis of cooperating groups, representatives from other groups such as labour were not invited to sit in Cabinet. Thus, the idea of group government was also shelved. The imperatives of a parliamentary system were brought home to the United Farmers very early in their reign. Although there is no doubt that they would have liked to put into practice their notions of how governments should run, they had perforce to settle down and govern just like the much-maligned, traditional old-line parties.

## Social Credit

Like the UFA before them, the Social Credit party was surprised to find itself at the political helm in Alberta in 1935. The movement led by William Aberhart began its life as a lobby group for the adoption of social credit principles propounded by Scottish engineer Major Clifford Douglas. It was only after the UFA government rejected Social Credit that Aberhart decided to run candidates in the 1935 provincial election.

Aberhart, often referred to as "Bible Bill," a lay preacher and principal of Crescent Heights High School, came to Calgary from Seaforth, Ontario in 1910. He was deeply affected when a despondent student committed suicide as a result of Depression-era conditions. Introduced to Social Credit at this time, he became its greatest promoter, weaving

---

2. Crerar was not averse to the Progressives working as a group and with the Liberals to achieve their legislative goals. However, Wood was adamant that Alberta Progressives would not betray their political principles for specific reforms. The Progressives were therefore a house divided.

the doctrine into his weekly religious broadcasts, the "Back to the Bible Hour," on CFCN Radio. His objective was to persuade the government to adopt Social Credit-style monetary reform to solve the devastating problems people were experiencing. When the UFA refused to do so, the impressive organization he had built up to popularize Social Credit was transformed into a political machine.

A reluctant entrant into the political fray and with its origins in religion, Social Credit was a movement rather than a political party. It did not claim to be a party and was thus able to denounce old-line parties. (Aberhart's denunciations extended to the "50 Big Shots," crooks, fornicators, and Central Canada.) He considered his efforts to convert the population to Social Credit a crusade and he saw nothing inappropriate in folding the political message into his weekly religious broadcasts. As Barr points out, "in 1935, when Aberhart promised to bring to government a non-partisan spirit unblemished by desire for personal gain and ties with hated eastern interests, he touched a very deep and responsive chord in many Albertans" (1974: 77). The attitude towards partisanship is also evident in Barr's comment that the disadvantage faced by the Liberals was that in the minds of thousands of Albertans, they were "politicians." Ernest Manning told a reporter from the *Edmonton Journal* that he would rather be doing his Bible work than his Cabinet duties and that "all of us entered into this in the spirit of a crusade. We are not politicians" (quoted in Barr, 1974: 86).

Aberhart proved to be ill-prepared in 1935, when Social Credit was swept into office and the UFA completely wiped off the political landscape. With 56 seats to the Liberals' five and two for the Conservatives, it was a decisive victory. Aritha van Herk comments that Aberhart was "almost dazed by what he wrought" on election night and the next day he asked a reporter for advice on political process "making it suddenly obvious that the persuasive preacher was utterly unprepared for what he was now faced with—keeping promises he had made to a ragged, struggling province" (2001: 249). That the new Premier felt unprepared for the job is confirmed by a conversation he had a few months later with Prime Minister Mackenzie King. Aberhart confided that "he did not know much about politics and hoped that he could call upon King at any time" (Elliott and Miller, 1987: 225).

During the next few years it became even clearer that Aberhart had

*Doreen Barrie*

little understanding of how things worked in the political realm.[3] The telegram sent to Douglas: "Victorious! When can you come?" reveals how overwhelmed Aberhart was. The founder of Social Credit had been appointed Reconstruction Advisor by the UFA government, so he had a contract with the province. Instead of coming to Alberta, he fired off numerous telegrams leading David Elliott to comment that it seemed "as if the people of Alberta were going to be governed by offshore telegrams" (Elliott: 2004: 113). As we shall see later, the consequences of Douglas' advice were far-reaching indeed.

Albertans became impatient when the government did not implement Social Credit measures, especially the much-anticipated $25 a month dividend. (Confident that they were to receive a cash infusion, some people booked cruises the day after the Social Credit victory.) Aberhart's popularity sagged and his equally impatient backbenchers threatened a revolt in 1937. He was then forced to allow the Social Credit Board, composed mainly of Douglasites in his caucus, to take control of government. According to Social Credit's theory of democracy, citizens have a right to demand certain policies but should leave to the experts and technicians how these outcomes would be realized. In other words, governments would be given a blank cheque. While one could visualize giving elected representatives a blank cheque (that is virtually what we do after every election) in this instance, Cabinet abdicated its responsibility to a Board composed of five private members (back benchers) who were authorized to appoint a commission of outside experts. Aberhart justified this by arguing that implementation of Social Credit would not be subject to political influence. This was an astonishing move as the government transferred its sovereign right to decide on important issues to a Board which got its advice from an unelected group (Bell, 1993: 118).

Most of the legislation drafted by the Social Credit Board was unsuccessful, either disallowed by the federal government, reserved by the Lieutenant-Governor or declared unconstitutional by the courts. These moves infuriated Aberhart and he excoriated the federal government,

---

3. He was aware of his strengths and, having kept the Education portfolio he set about reforming the education system in the province. By all accounts his reforms were good and well received.

taking his revenge by closing Government House, the official residence of the Lieutenant-Governor, an Ottawa appointee, and depriving him of his official car.

Social Credit certainly did not behave like an orthodox political party. With only seven opposition members, partisanship was hardly an issue and, in any case, Aberhart had little time for the legislature. In fact, he hardly ever spoke there (his detractors claimed it was because people could talk back), but he continued his Sunday broadcasts, suggesting that his religious following was more important to him. Perhaps the radio programs were meant to be a substitute for the legislature because they contained a confusing mixture of religion and politics.

In a nod to populism, one of the first pieces of legislation the Aberhart government passed was the Recall Act legislation which allowed constituents to recall (fire) their MLAs. Dissatisfied by his performance, Aberhart's own constituents initiated a petition to recall him and obtained the required 67% of signatures. There were charges that voters from outside the constituency had signed the petition just to get at Aberhart. The Act was repealed and the Premier held on to his seat.

When he became Premier, Ernest Manning, the reluctant but astute politician, did carry on with his Bible work and his non-partisanship manifested itself in his devotion to religion. In its annual report in 1947, the Social Credit Board questioned the need for political parties and argued for non-partisan "leagues of electors" (Barr, 1949: 129). Pal states that the province "had a curiously apolitical public life" and Manning's views on partisanship are made explicit in a White Paper on Human Resources Development presented to the legislature in 1967:

> The paper is non-partisan… If the time and energy currently spent on political manoeuvring for partisan advantage, were instead channelled into a supreme and constructive effort to solve the problems and meet the challenges confronting the nation, Canadians would not only be happier but infinitely further ahead (quoted in Pal, 1992: 18).

Although Social Credit made no attempt to implement delegate democracy or referenda, the recall legislation suggests that the Party was responding to some impulse in the population. However, the depth of its commitment is revealed in the speed with which the legislation was dropped.

## Progressive Conservatives

When Peter Lougheed brought the long Social Credit era to an end in 1971, it was the first time in half a century that a "traditional, old-line party" was in office. The expectation was that the Progressive Conservative Party would adopt the partisan tactics utilized by its counterparts in the rest of the country. However, in true Alberta fashion, Lougheed eschewed partisanship.

His term in office coincided with bitter battles with Ottawa over oil and gas as well as the constitution, and in these disputes, he presented his government as the champion of provincial rights, a stance guaranteed to mobilize the entire population behind him. With lopsided majorities in the Alberta legislature it was easy to ignore opposition parties, to appeal to Albertans directly and claim to represent the public interest. He was impatient with opposition, dividing the population into "do-ers" and "knockers," the former category comprising those supporting his agenda and the latter those who were against it. Tupper points out that his government was "based on strong executive leadership and appeal to non-partisanship, that is the hallmark of Alberta's political culture" (2004: 234).

As the bulk of Lougheed's battles were with the federal government, Alberta's arch-enemy, to criticize the Premier was regarded as disloyalty to the province. Opposition parties were thus in an untenable position: either fall behind the government or oppose its position and run the risk of having their allegiance to Alberta questioned. Unable to take the latter position, they were forced to agree with the government, thus making them seem redundant. That they adopted the right position is evident from the response of Albertans to a question in a survey during the Lougheed era. When asked if opposition parties should support the government in disputes with the federal government, 73% of the sample agreed (Gibbins, 1979: 162). In the 1982 election, the Conservative slogan which appeared on all signage was "For Alberta" implying that the province needed to present a united front to Ottawa. Stevenson points out that the Premier made this explicit towards the end of the campaign when he stated that Prime Minister Trudeau would be happy if too many opposition candidates were elected (1985: 281).

Leslie Pal contends that Lougheed became a master of non-partisan leadership, but Don Getty's non-partisan pose was not very successful given that he faced a much stronger opposition (1992: 20). The unfortunate Don Getty, Lougheed's successor, had to pick up the pieces when the Alberta economy went bust in the mid-1980s. He also had to deal with a healthy (for Alberta!) contingent of 22 opposition members in the 83-member legislature.

When Ralph Klein assumed power in 1993, he immediately set about reducing the deficit, a campaign in which he encouraged all Albertans to participate by tightening their belts. He, too, appealed to the population above the heads of the opposition parties, inviting the people to become "part of the solution rather than part of the problem." Although there were 32 Liberals in the legislature, their leader, Laurence Decore, had a serious problem. He had been hammering away on the need to attack the deficit while the Conservatives played down the problem. In fact Decore used to travel around with a "deficit clock" which kept track of how rapidly the deficit was growing. Deficit reduction became the main plank in the Liberal election platform, but Klein belatedly embraced it, taking some wind out of Liberal sails. Thus the two parties were prescribing the same medicine: either massive cuts or brutal cuts.

After the 1993 election the Liberals could hardly reverse their position on the issue, so they merely echoed the Conservative line—thus rendering their message redundant. They could criticize the speed of cost cutting and some of the targets, but apart from that they were marginalized, enabling the Conservatives to ignore them. Opposition came from outside the legislature (from groups that were easy to label "special interests"), once again underlining the superfluity of partisanship.

Like other Alberta Premiers, Klein prefers to avoid the legislature, pointing out that being in Edmonton brings on an attack of "Dome disease," a reference to the dome on the legislative building. He has often expressed a preference for connecting with people directly rather than interacting with their elected representatives. Legislative sessions have averaged 48 days per year between 1998 and 2004 (ranging from a high of 63 days in 1998 to 36 in 2004). In contrast, annual sitting days for the House of Commons range from 135 to 200 (Brownsey, 2005: 33). As opposition parties get most of their publicity during legislative sittings, it is little wonder they are marginalized and the non-partisan nature of politics is reinforced.

There have been many battles with the federal government since

Klein was elected; this too is a familiar strategy to deflect attention outwards to the *real* opposition.

## Natural Resources

If there is one issue that ignites passions in Alberta it is natural resources. It would be difficult to exaggerate the sense of injustice Albertans feel about the fact that the federal government retained ownership of natural resources in 1905. I am not denying that this action was discriminatory, but the Prairies were in a unique position: none of the prairie provinces had been self-governing colonies prior to 1867. Manitoba's elevation to provincehood (in 1870) was fast-tracked because Louis Riel forced Ottawa's hand. Had the Métis leader not done so, Manitoba too would likely have become a province in 1905. Arguably, Manitobans should have been the most aggrieved as they had to wait 60 years to be granted control of their land and resources.

At the time of Confederation, there was no real fear that the American army would march in and occupy any of the colonies—the Fenians (disgruntled Irishmen who wanted to rid the continent of the British) hardly posed a threat. The sparsely populated prairie provinces did constitute a prize for the Americans because western settlement in the US was far advanced and there was no free land left. Alberta was the last agricultural frontier on the continent; Saskatchewan and Manitoba were only slightly ahead. Ottawa was interested in the land but the resources thereon and thereunder were of little interest.

I suspect few Albertans are aware of Ottawa's indifference to the province's resources in 1905—an example of what ended up on the cutting floor of Alberta's history. Another little-known fact is that the prairie provinces received a generous annual grant from Ottawa in compensation for alienation of the resources.

Dissatisfaction with the region's colonial status was shared by the other prairie provinces, but natural resources occupy a special place in the pantheon of irritants for Alberta because of subsequent battles.

### Liberals

Although negotiations had begun to effect a transfer of control over natural resources during the Liberal regime, there was little progress. Given that the Rutherford government was preoccupied with setting up the infrastructure and dealing with the railway scandal, it should come as no surprise that this was not a priority. Sifton had to deal with the fallout from the scandal and then World War I intervened. Thus, natural resource ownership was on the back burner until the 1920s.

## The UFA

Agreement on handing over control of natural resources to Alberta seemed imminent in 1922, but a dispute over the details delayed the transfer until 1930. This achievement by Premier John Brownlee was very popular in the province, but there was no immediate move to exploit the province's resources. The major debate at the time revolved around hydroelectric power, that is, whether Spray Lakes, west of Calgary, should be developed as a public utility. Although there was a demand at the 1930 UFA convention that the province develop the newly-acquired resources based on the principles of public ownership "and that immediate action be taken to prevent private industry from acquiring a monopoly on power sites," the province allowed Calgary Power, then a private company, to develop the site (Kooyman, 1980: 80–81). It would be a while before the provincial government played a larger role in the energy industry.

## Social Credit

The story of the modern oil industry begins in 1947 with Leduc #1, when the well came in with a roar on February 13, triggering the province's biggest resource boom. What is less well known is that oil and gas were first discovered in Turner Valley in 1914 but production was modest. As a result of these earlier strikes, there was frantic activity in the valley leading to rapid depletion of the field. Richards and Pratt (1979: 46–47) point out that the province watched helplessly as vast quantities of gas (rates as high as 600 million cubic feet a day) were flared by small independent companies, as there was no market for it at that time. Royalite (an Imperial Oil subsidiary) had an exclusive contract with Calgary's gas utility, so the small companies did not get a look in. Thus for 14 years Albertans watched a precious resource going up in smoke before the Alberta government was able to intervene successfully. The "law of the jungle" prevailed and there were no enforceable conservation laws.

The indifference of the federal government to this potentially lucrative resource is demonstrated in its failure to act despite the issue being brought to its notice by conservationists in the late 1920s (Richards and Pratt, 1979: 47).

The colossal waste in Turner Valley eventually led Aberhart's government, in 1938, to the establish the Oil and Gas Conservation Board (later the Energy Resources Conservation Board) which was the precursor to today's Energy Utilities Board. Practices in the petroleum industry forced the Social Credit government to set about easing the chaotic situation in Turner Valley and to turn to American precedents to address Alberta's problems.

If Ottawa's negligence over natural resources prior to 1930 was a concern, it was the fear of federal interference that prompted the Social Credit government to take pre-emptive measures to insulate the natural gas industry. The orgy of waste in "Hell's Half Acre" produced a very protective attitude towards natural gas in the province. A strongly worded editorial in the *Lethbridge Herald* in the summer of 1949 summed up prevailing sentiments:

> Albertans want no wastage of this invaluable resource. There has been too much wastage already in the Turner Valley. The flares that lighted the skies for years over the Valley told their own story. Most of our communities want natural gas for fuel. The demand for this clean fuel is growing and the Herald wants to see our needs guarded. If [export] is allowed it should be permitted only under strict control and not for the enrichment of absentee capitalists who have no real interest in the country (quoted in Richards and Pratt, 1979: 64).

Natural gas was seen as a potential catalyst to industrial development, doing for Alberta what hydroelectric power had done for Quebec and Ontario. The Manning government's main fear was of federal intrusion, but shortages within the province were also a concern, so it took drastic steps to prevent either eventuality. Manning set up Alberta Gas Trunk Lines (with an ingenious structure that would prevent any group from gaining control) as a single gas gathering system within the province. The fear was that Ottawa's jurisdiction would extend right up to the wellhead via federally incorporated pipeline companies operating throughout the province. The solution was that Alberta Gas Trunk Lines would, through a network of pipelines, have a monopoly over gas gathering within provincial boundaries and would distribute the gas to companies like Trans-Canada at the provincial border (Richards and Pratt, 1979: 66–67).

To address the issue of possible shortages, the Conservation Board was empowered to authorize removal of gas from Alberta only if there were proven reserves for the use of Albertans for 30 years. The "Alberta First" policy was regarded as a reasonable one since Albertans considered natural gas their birthright. This policy no longer exists.

Manning's initiatives were defensive, anticipating that Ottawa might force exports and interfere in the natural gas industry. There was some justification for this fear because federal Trade and Commerce Minister C.D. Howe had pressured the province to export gas to the Pacific Northwest (Richards and Pratt, 1979: 65). However, the Social Credit government's actions were also conditioned by memories of federal control for the first quarter-century of the province's existence.

Peter Lougheed will go down in the annals of Alberta history as the Premier who put Alberta on the map. It was during his first term in office that OPEC began to flex its muscles and quadrupled the price of oil. In the ensuing dispute with the federal government over the price of oil in Canada, Lougheed adopted a strong provincial rights stance, challenging Prime Minister Trudeau's more centralist position.

Perhaps the nadir in federal-provincial relations was imposition of the National Energy Program (NEP) in 1980. More than any federal action before or since, the NEP seemed to confirm Alberta's assigned place in Confederation: supplier of resources to Central Canada, in this case Ontario. The NEP was unveiled a quarter of a century ago, and it is certainly less salient for my students today, but in 1980 many Albertans were incandescent with rage. Some are still smouldering.

When Ottawa unilaterally set the price of a very precious provincial resource, many Albertans were stunned and some contemplated separation. As far as the Alberta government was concerned, the NEP was just the culmination of federal actions spanning almost a decade. For years, Alberta had reluctantly agreed to keep the domestic price of oil lower than the world price even though it deprived the province of revenue from a depleting resource. Imposition of an export tax on oil was clearly discriminatory, as no other resource, whether hydroelectric power, lumber or minerals, was subject to such a tax.

Reaction to the NEP from the Alberta government was swift and effective. Two days after it was unveiled, Lougheed spoke to Albertans on television and, using very emotive language described Alberta's plan of action: he announced that the province would turn down the taps, reducing production by 60,000 barrels a day in three stages and halt the construction of new tar sands plants. He reminded Albertans about the 25-year struggle to become like the other provinces, referred to the threatened "patrimony" of the province, and accused Ottawa of "walking into our home and occupying the living room." It was a speech designed to revisit old grievances and evoke an emotional reaction, which it did.

The Premier knew he was tapping into a very deep vein of dissatisfaction in the province. Discriminatory treatment towards a depleting resource raised serious questions about ownership and whether the transfer of resources in 1930 was really complete. He was also reviving memories of slights experienced by Albertans who had tried to raise capital in Central Canada but were turned down, Albertans who felt patronized by Ontarians and all those who were suspicious of Ottawa's motives.

Given the temper of the times, it was easy for the population to believe that incentives to explore on "Canada lands"[4] were to "get at" Alberta. Albertans were unaware that when the Conservatives came to power the major oil companies were not developing their leases because they felt that the western sedimentary basin had reached a point of maturity where returns had begun to decline (Richards & Pratt, 1979: 124). The Lougheed government had to provide drilling incentives to those companies that actually undertook to explore for crude oil to ensure activity in the oil patch. Albertans were too angry to appreciate that Ottawa needed revenue to subsidize offshore imports that were being utilized east of Ontario. Even the Alberta government acknowledged this. (Alberta's revenue on a barrel of oil was well over 37% of the price in 1975). Albertans were infuriated at the injustice of the NEP and wondered why it was silent on other forms of energy such as hydroelectric power.[5]

---

4. This refers to land that belongs to the federal government by virtue of being offshore or in the Arctic.
5. When I lecture on the NEP in class, I feel I should first don a bullet-proof vest. However, when students hear the rationale for the Program from the federal side and Alberta's objections to it, they are quite surprised.

The NEP provides a textbook example of how provincial governments (not only in Alberta) can summon outrage and support in battles with the federal government. Former Premier Glen Clark of British Columbia engaged in much "fed-bashing" to shore up his government which had a slim majority. The strategy is employed to this day.

The contemporary analogue to the NEP is the Kyoto Accord. As burning of fossil fuels contributes to greenhouse gas emissions, any attempt to curb emissions will naturally affect production and consumption of these forms of energy which are Alberta's bread, butter and jam. Despite initial majority support for the Accord in the province, after the Klein government launched a concerted attack on it, public opinion turned around. The Kyoto Accord was labeled the "Son of NEP" as a reminder of the vulnerability of Alberta's petroleum resources. The provincial government even retained Peter Lougheed to advise on a possible constitutional challenge.

## Suspicion of Banks

The farming community was heavily in debt in the 1920s following expansion when wheat prices were high. When prices fell they had difficulty making their payments and called on the government for help. Even more serious was a prolonged drought in the southeastern part of the province which began in 1917, long before the UFA came to office. By 1923 it had caused the worst farm abandonment in Canadian history, also resulting in the collapse of the Union Bank and a sharp decline in the number of loan companies from 25 to four (Jones, 2004: 64). Those who had to walk away from their property did not feel very charitable towards financial institutions which were located in Eastern Canada.

Faced with crippling debt and a UFA government that seemed reluctant to take measures to alleviate the problem, the farming community was furious. Social Credit's success can be attributed, in part, to Aberhart's denunciation of banks, which was music to farmers' ears. The proposal to establish Treasury Branches, in effect provincial banks, was very popular with the population.

Albertans have a touching faith in home-grown financial institutions, believing that they will be more understanding and sympathetic than those based in Central Canada. When the Canadian Commercial

Bank and Northland Bank collapsed in 1985 it was a blow to provincial pride. However, the Principal Group's failure two years later was particularly painful as thousands of Albertans lost their life savings. The province's regulator should probably have stepped in earlier but was reluctant to do so. Some critics believe there was political interference as the government of the day did not want another Alberta financial institution to fail.

What the foregoing has demonstrated is that certain pivotal events in the province's history have influenced the Alberta psyche. Non-partisanship is not invoked directly any more but manifests itself in the way the governing party treats the opposition in the legislature. It is visible in the preference for a consensus and compromise. Successive Premiers have "risen above" petty political squabbles and given the impression that they are implementing the general will. Politics is derided—in fact an Alberta MP once remarked that the trouble with the House of Commons is that it is too political! Albertans have seldom had a healthy opposition party in the legislature and many are therefore unconvinced about the need for one.

Attitudes towards real or perceived federal interference in natural resources in the province still elicits a strong response.

The central question is whether the formative events and their reinforcement over the decades have produced a population that differs significantly from Canadians elsewhere. To establish that, we need to take a look at the values and attitudes that prevail in other parts of the country; this will be the subject of the next chapter.

# 3

# Political Culture

It is a mistake to assume that Albertans are detached, prefer to remain aloof or even to separate, along with their wealth, from the rest of Canada. Citizens of federal states have dual loyalties and, given the strength of regional sentiment in the province, it is often assumed that in Alberta most people would think of themselves as Albertans first. In fact, only 16% of the population sees themselves primarily as Albertans (Dyck, 2000: 214). This suggests that Albertans, like most other Canadians, see themselves as part of a larger national community and, as we shall see, they share fundamental values with that community.[1] Developments in the last few decades have wrought such sweeping changes that the notion of a national community, indeed even of the nation state, is in question. The world is increasingly interconnected, borders are more porous, products and ideas flow easily in and out of countries and people are more mobile than they have ever been. An interesting question in such a fluid environment is: what is the glue that binds the people of a country together? What is it that distinguishes Canadians from, say, Americans or Germans? In the context of this book, a related question is: what distinguishes Albertans from people in other parts of Canada?

---

1. Only in Newfoundland did a majority of the population identify themselves in terms of their provincial identity.

The most obvious tie is that citizens of a country are subject to a unique set of laws and entitlements. Unless a country is relatively young, the population will also share a history and numerous experiences. Perhaps the strongest bond is a common set of values and attitudes which provides the raw materials for public policy in that country. The goal of this chapter is to describe the values Canadians subscribe to and which influence the way people respond to their political universe. These are deeply held and widely shared values that must be distinguished from opinions on contemporary issues, which can be very transitory. Opinion formation will be dealt with in Chapter 6.

## Political Culture

The concept political scientists use to describe the value consensus that exists in a society is political culture. It is the foundation or reservoir of values, attitudes and beliefs that is shared by people in a particular society and which influences the way in which they make judgements about political issues.[2] Many variables influence how political messages are received, but at the most fundamental level political culture is the determining factor. This store of values often grows out of shared experiences, a common history and a set of myths and symbols that stitch the population together. It is not possible in this book to delve too deeply into the extensive material on the subject of political culture in Canada. However, it is essential to have a rudimentary background on this concept, as it is central to the argument of this book that, at one level, Albertans share a political culture with other Canadians. Although there are facets of Alberta's political culture that are unique, my argument in this chapter is that there is a set of fundamental values that is shared across the country.

---

2. These are the building blocks of a political system. They provide the underlying assumptions and unspoken rules that govern behaviour and expectations within a political community. A political culture is like an umbrella under which more than one ideology may coexist. For instance, Canada's political culture is believed to consist of a mixture of conservatism, liberalism and socialism (Horowitz, 1970). The values and attitudes are reflected in political institutions, sustained by political symbols and perpetuated by political socialization. Thus, there is a reciprocal relationship among the elements (Barrie, 1980).

SOURCE: ARTIZANS.COM

*Ralph Klein takes aim at Kyoto (cartoon first appeared in the Edmonton* Journal).

Political culture sets limits on what is acceptable, what will "fly" in a particular society, but it is not a straitjacket which leaves no room to manoeuvre. There is a range of possible options to tackle a particular issue, and there could be virulent disagreement among different segments of the population as to which is the correct one. Disagreement on issues like same-sex marriage, the Kyoto Accord and whether governments should provide loan guarantees to private corporations are examples of the vast array of matters on which there are differing views. However, agreement is eventually reached in the political arena.

Gurston Dacks sums this point up nicely in his comment that political culture provides the setting but not the script (1985: 87). We articulate our values via discussion in coffee shops, on talk shows and around the kitchen table. Such discussions revolve around the pros and cons of proposals or assessments of government actions. We might argue about whether the government should commit more money to the military or whether oil companies should be charged higher royalties. Without being aware of it, people reveal their values and draw on important symbols in these discussions. These assessments about political actions are based primarily on how people see the role of the state: should the state loom large in our lives or behave more like a referee? Whether the state should play a central role or a cameo will be determined by the political culture of a particular society.

Before exploring Canadian political culture, it is important to clarify how I will be using certain terms. One of the occupational hazards of being in the social sciences is that one is confronted daily with terminology which is used very loosely in the media and in everyday speech. Terms that might mean something specific to a social scientist are often used quite differently in the "vernacular." More importantly, the popular usage becomes the accepted usage. As we shall see, the word "conservative" is a prime example of this tendency. That is why it will be useful to discuss the different "isms" and explain how they are understood by political scientists.

The ideological spectrum in the western world developed in a sort of progression, tracking major changes in society.[3] In other words, a particular set of ideas provided the foundation that underpinned the status quo. Thus the feudal/tory era was supported by attitudes that reflected and reinforced such values as elitism, paternalism, support for tradition and a belief that the group is more important than the individual. A tory (i.e., a conservative) is someone who conserves, who does not embrace change with enthusiasm. The term also describes someone who believes that each of us has a place in the social hierarchy with a prescribed role. Thus some are born to lead and others to follow and, for the most part, both parties are comfortable with and accept their position in the hierarchy.

Liberalism represents a rejection of tory values. It is in fact the antithesis of conservatism. It is egalitarian and places great emphasis on

---

3. To summarize the evolution of ideologies in a few paragraphs necessitates a gross over-simplification of an extremely complex topic. Scholars have written volumes on the subject. For our purposes, this stripped-down treatment will have to suffice.

freedom of action (e.g. to practise any religion, speak freely and associate with anyone) and freedom from certain actions of others (e.g. discriminatory treatment). Liberals are firm believers in liberty and in the primacy of the individual. The new liberal values followed the emancipation of the merchant class which challenged the hegemony of aristocrats. Liberal values accompanied the rise of the capitalist system, so liberals favour small government and minimal interference in the marketplace.

Socialism contains elements of both its predecessors and is thus a synthesis of the other two philosophies. It emphasizes the importance of group interests as does conservatism, but rejects the latter's elitism. Like liberals, socialists are egalitarian; but unlike liberals, they believe in a positive state—i.e., one that intervenes in society to redistribute wealth and to play a role in ensuring fairness for the disadvantaged.[4]

This brief foray into the evolution of ideologies reveals the wide gap between popular usage of such labels and the older definitions. The reader will immediately pick up that the description of conservatives does not fit with contemporary notions of conservatives or neo-conservatives. What is now referred to as neo-conservatism is in fact a combination of classical liberalism and elements of conservatism. Individuals who are called "fiscal conservatives" favour small government, do not support government intervention unless it is absolutely necessary, and expect governments to balance the books. (To complicate this matter even further, fiscal conservatives are sometimes called "neo-liberals"!) The term "social conservative" is applied to those who, among other things, support traditional family values and traditional gender roles. They oppose abortion and same-sex marriage and favour capital punishment.

Not many people fit neatly into the packages which have distinctive ideological labels. One of the exercises my students had to do for a course was to slot themselves into one of the ideological boxes.

---

4. This brief discussion on the three major ideologies does not touch on strands within each one. For instance, there are liberals and conservatives who hold views that tend towards socialism and socialists whose views include liberal or conservative ideals. In addition, one could argue environmentalism is poised to takes its place in the ideological pantheon and if it does it will represent a rejection of liberalism. The place of nationalism is problematic. In Quebec, for example, ideological predispositions are clouded by nationalism as the latter trumps ideology in some instances.

Interestingly, they felt ideologically challenged because most of them found their beliefs spilled out untidily, blurring the line between the categories. They were reassured to hear that ideological coherence is quite unusual, that most of us are a blend of the three major ideologies with other systems of thought creeping in as well. In fact, this lack of ideological "purity" is a feature of Canadian political culture. Nevertheless, there is widespread agreement that Canadians are basically liberal in their orientation—i.e., in terms of the preference for freedom and a judicious amount of individualism. Bell and Tepperman sum up the prevailing view in their observation that liberalism is "the ideology of the dominant class; it has the full force of the state, Church, media and educational system behind it; it has been trained into all of us" (1981: 232).

## Canadian Political Culture

Despite the dominant position of liberalism mentioned above, Canadian political culture is believed to consist of a mixture of liberal, tory and socialist values. Canada is often compared with the US, a thoroughly liberal country with no tory or socialist strands in its political culture. Many Canadians are irritated at the tendency to compare ourselves so frequently with our neighbours to the south. This is partly because these comparisons tend to make judgements about which country is "superior." Nevertheless, because the United States looms so large on our horizon, is so powerful and shares a language with (most of) us, it is not surprising. It is also useful to have a yardstick against which to measure ourselves.

American sociologist S.M. Lipset (1970), a scholar who compared the two societies, argued that the differences between Canada and the United States could be attributed to formative events in the history of the two countries. Canada's was a natural birth: there was no dramatic rupture in relations with Britain. In the case of the US it was more like a caesarian section, with a decisive break, the War of Independence, that brought the country into existence. Lipset refers to the two events as a revolution (in the US) and counter-revolution (in Canada). These defining moments left an indelible mark on each society, resulting in the rejection of the British value system in the US and its retention in Canada. Consequently, one sees a continuation of British institutions and value patterns north of the border. The gradual evolution of the

Canadian identity also contributes to the difficulty in articulating in a clear-cut, unequivocal way, what Canadians stand for.

In a later work Lipset (1990) returns to the Canada-US comparison, reaffirming his contention that Canadian society is characterized by hierarchy, elitism and deference. As a result, he contends, Canadians are more class-conscious, have more respect for authority and greater deference to elites. In contrast, Americans are egalitarian and more ready to challenge authority. Quoting surveys done in both countries over two decades (from the late 1960s to the late 1980s), Lipset shows that Canadians favour a much stronger role for government than do Americans (1990: 140–42).

This can be seen in the previous reliance on Crown corporations in Canada in the past and more generally in the mixed economy. In the last decade or so many Crown corporations have been sold to the private sector but whether this signals a shift in the attitude of ordinary Canadians towards a mixed economy remains to be seen. The Canadian health care system, with its universal accessibility, would be a prime example of the preference for adopting a collective approach to addressing important social issues. In fact, some argue that health care has become a metaphor for what it means to be a Canadian.

If there is one characteristic that differentiates the two countries, it is individualism. This is the wellspring from which many other key values flow. The strong commitment to individualism as a defining value in the US is reflected in the preference for competition, individual economic freedom and a relatively small public sector. Canadians are also individualistic (especially when compared with European countries), but their individualism is tempered by robust support for collective solutions and pooling risk. The roots of this value are believed to lie in the French feudal system and the influx of United Empire Loyalists who moved to Canada after the American Revolution.

Some also argue that Canada's geography and climate necessitate cooperation and a larger role for government. Historically, Canadians have held a more benevolent view of government than Americans. Political scientist Philip Resnick argues that "[w]hat differentiates Canadians from Americans is the fact that Canadians remain a good deal more European in their sensibilities and will continue to be the more European part of North America into the foreseeable future"

(2005: 76). When compared with other developed countries, Canada falls in the middle on such indicators as level of social expenditures or government revenue and expenditure as a percentage of Gross Domestic Product, with the US much further down the list.

Political culture is not static: it evolves slowly unless some dramatic event in a country's history, such as the American revolution, provokes a rejection of the values the previous regime espoused. Here in Canada, we have not had a similar transformative experience—but that does not mean our value system is immutable. For instance, the decisive rejection of the Charlottetown Accord in 1992 despite solid support from political and social elites suggests a weakening of the longstanding deference to them. Recent analysis has confirmed this decline in deference (Nevitte, 1996).

Changing values in advanced industrial states have been observed in cross-national studies conducted by political scientist Ronald Inglehart (2000). Inglehart has conducted extensive surveys over several years and argues that he has detected a pattern of systematic change in values among people in advanced industrial societies The thrust of his argument is that the generation brought up in the post-World War II period has enjoyed a prolonged period of prosperity. Consequently, as individuals in this age cohort have not experienced economic insecurity, their priorities are "post material." In other words, quality of life issues are more important than economic security, self-expression trumps deference to elites, and cultural diversity is not considered threatening.

Inglehart further contends that there is a questioning of hierarchical, centralized bureaucratic institutions, and that concerns for the environment and women's rights characterize the priorities of young people (2000). Inglehart has his critics who have questioned his thesis and methodology as well as the applicability of his findings to some countries, but there is some evidence that his findings hold true in Canada.

A couple of years ago, the *Globe and Mail* (Anderssen, Valpy et al., 2004) commissioned research on Canadian attitudes on a range of issues and focused primarily on young Canadians. Their findings provided an interesting glimpse into the future. The views expressed by the twenty-somethings fit very neatly into the post-materialist/post-modern mould identified by Inglehart. Among this age cohort, quality of life issues are important, multiculturalism is mentioned approvingly and there is acceptance of all types of diversity. If the *Globe*'s research is accurate, and there is evidence from other sources that bears it out, the younger generation is cosmopolitan and eager to play a role on a much wider stage. That they are not regional in their outlook may have some implications for federal-provincial relations in the future.

In fact, young Canadians do not have a great deal of faith or trust in governments. Voter turnout among young Canadians is low (although it went up during the 2004 federal election campaign thanks to aggressive attempts improve the figure) and participation in political parties lower still. This phenomenon is not unique to Canada, as political parties in Europe are having an equally difficult time attracting young voters.

Disenchantment with mainstream political activity and declining trust in government among all voters has been noted in other advanced industrial countries. However, there are unique Canadian experiences that have contributed to the situation in this country. For roughly three decades beginning in the mid-1970s Canadian politics has been tumultuous.

The election of a separatist party in Quebec and the energy crisis plunged the country into a round of constitutional discussions that culminated in the 1982 Constitution Act and the Charter of Rights. Entrenchment of the Charter was hailed as a tremendous achievement in the English-speaking provinces. Unfortunately, the Quebec government did not "sign on" to the new constitution, dampening the euphoria about severing the last link with Britain. There were two abortive attempts to obtain Quebec's support which did nothing to bring harmony to the country. The response in Quebec was a second referendum on sovereignty in 1995, which came within a whisker of gaining majority support. In addition, there was a very divisive debate on free trade with the United States during the 1988 election and a bitter battle to stop the Goods & Services Tax. Prime Minister Mulroney's popularity, at 16%, hit an historic low. The combination of these shocks had an impact on the way the Canadian public viewed their governments and it also shattered the party system.

The 1993 election saw the rise of the Reform Party and huge gains for the newly formed Bloc Québecois. The former, which espoused populist ideals such as citizen initiatives, referendums and recall of MPs, seemed to fit the mood of dissatisfaction with representative government. Although a regional party, its populism was attractive to a population weary of governments that seemed to pay little attention to voters except at election time.

Given the tumult of the last three decades, it would be surprising if Canadian attitudes remained constant. There was greater resentment about paying taxes and calls for tax cuts. However, after severe cutbacks to social programs, especially health care, there were few calls for further tax cuts. That Canadians remain committed to a national community is apparent from the level of support for equalization payments which are made to have-not provinces. In November 2004, the Centre for Research and Information on Canada found that 85% of Canadians supported equalization payments. Support was lowest in Alberta but was still at a healthy 78%.

In this new millennium, Canadians appear much less sanguine about the capacity of governments to provide answers to social problems. Trust in government has declined, particularly in the wake of revelations surrounding public money being misused following the last Quebec referendum. It remains to be seen whether this is a long-term trend or whether another political leader can restore faith in political institutions and practices.

In my opinion, Canadians are pragmatic people who lowered their expectations of government because of large deficits, but I have my doubts that they have abandoned the commitment to levelling the playing field for less fortunate members of society. Even if there is a permanent shift in Canadian values, it is most likely that it has taken place across the country, although to a lesser extent in Quebec. The people of Quebec see the provincial government as guardian of the French language and culture, so the role of the provincial state at the very least will continue to be strong. In addition, many Quebecers are social democrats.

## Regional Differences

Some scholars who have studied political culture contend that we can speak of regional political cultures or sub-cultures—in fact, that we can view each province as having a distinct political culture (Simeon and Elkins, 1974; Wilson, 1974). However, the measures they used were not designed to tap into the core values to which I am referring.

This is not to argue, however, that regional differences do not exist. They do, but their extent is often over-stated. Each province has a different mix in its population and resource base and enjoys a different style and quality of life. Each province also has a unique political history which influences the way in which its citizens assess the impact of policies, especially those emanating from Ottawa. Citizens must perforce "think provincially," as they have provincial health care cards, automobile licences and labour laws. It is in the political history of a province that one will find important symbols that speak only to the people of that province. We have seen how historical events influence the views of Albertans. However, to argue that provincial boundaries encapsulate differing views of the world at a fundamental level is to exaggerate regional differences. In analytical terms it is convenient to divide the country neatly along provincial lines. Sometimes we (academics) collapse the country into five regions (Atlantic, Quebec, Ontario, the Prairies and BC, often ignoring the Territories!), as five is a more manageable number and the groupings make some sense. However, when Canadians are asked to define their own regions, they do so in a most idiosyncratic way, which confounds the categories researchers work with!

Region has salience in Canadian politics and Western Canadians have legitimate grievances that contribute to regional sentiment. To a large extent, western alienation flows from being on the periphery. Children in the West learn at their mother's knee how the region has suffered at the hands of Ottawa and Central Canada. The sense of injustice which is sometimes reinforced by Western Canadian politicians makes it relatively easy to appeal to regional angst to garner support.

A recent study came to the conclusion that "the traditional emphasis on regional variations in Canadian political culture is overstated, and perpetuating the search for regional distinctiveness risks missing the forest for the trees" (quoted in Lawson, 2005: 141).

It is important to distinguish between regional interests, primarily regional economic interests, and attitudes towards major policy issues. As regional variation is neither strong nor consistent on such matters, one could safely say that a set of shared Canadian values does exist.

The foregoing discussion is an attempt to show that one can speak of a pan-Canadian set of values. When we examine Alberta political culture, it will become obvious that the perception of differences between

Albertans and other Canadians is exaggerated if not inaccurate. Yet, as we shall see, constant repetition has lent credence to these putative differences and they have become part of the Alberta folklore.

Before tackling Alberta political culture, we will take a look at some common misconceptions about the province.

# 4

## Perceptions and Misperceptions

The argument made in the previous chapter is that a pan-Canadian political culture does exist. However, its existence is obscured by perceptions of the general public and analyses which suggest that regional diversity includes political subcultures in the different regions or even in each province. As each provincial jurisdiction is a container, the tendency is to look for differences rather than to find similarities. Political scientist Roger Gibbins has observed that regionalism "may be more salient to political elites than to mass publics... A regionalized political system need not rest upon a foundation of a regionalized political culture" (1982: 176). This chapter will explore perceptions about Albertans, painting two pictures of this province: one the negative portrait that no one would want to hang in the living room, and the other a self-portrait that is overly flattering.

The negative stereotype of Albertans which admittedly is a trifle overdrawn does, I think, reflect the tenor of opinion in some parts of the country. It is certainly visible in media coverage of the province.[1] Many

---

1. A few years ago *Vancouver Sun* columnist Barbara Yaffe wrote a flattering piece about Calgary after a visit to the city. Stating that Calgary is a modern, vibrant city, she then

Albertans, including myself, have experienced glimmers of this view-point not just in Central Canada but even in the West. It would be fair to say that most Albertans are seen as unsophisticated cowboys, as right-wing rednecks who care little about their fellow Canadians. They are also painted as social conservatives who, at the very least, are uncomfortable with homosexuals, and at worst are homophobes. In addition, it is assumed that they oppose abortion and gun control, favour capital punishment and are anti-Semitic.

The affluence enjoyed by the province is also believed to have produced a right-wing mindset with an appetite for tax cuts and a minimal role for government. Alberta comes across as a perennial malcontent, dissatisfied with its place in Confederation. Referring to lopsided majorities in the legislature, the oft-repeated comment is that Alberta does not have elections, it has stampedes. We will explore the question of one-party dominance to see if this makes the province unique.

The self-perception of Albertans is equally questionable. As mentioned earlier, there is a very different view within the province, a much more positive one. The painted-in-Alberta portrait is very flattering: a population of rugged individualists who worked hard for the wealth we possess (including the natural wealth!), are self reliant, entrepreneurial and innovative.[2] The Lougheed government claimed to be the last bastion of free enterprise in the country. (Perhaps it felt like that because the other three western provinces had NDP governments in the early 1970s.) There is also a sense that the province has been unfairly treated for a century and is currently being stripped of its wealth by Ottawa. We will deal with the Alberta self-perception in the chapter on construction of an identity.

---

commented that in the 1980s people used to drive around the downtown area in trucks with rifles in the back! This is just one example of many in which journalists make reference to the Wild West when they refer to the province or to Calgary specifically.

2. Some people mention with pride that Alberta has a higher proportion of people working than any other province. The implication is that Albertans are imbued with the work ethic unlike people elsewhere. However, there are two variables that contribute to this: Alberta has a relatively young population and the unemployment rate is low because the economy is booming. Secondly, young people are migrating here from other regions to find work. People are migrating to BC as well, but many are seniors who wish to enjoy the more clement weather.

SOURCE: GLENBOW ARCHIVES M-8000-1291

*Calgarians enjoy dressing western during the Calgary Exhibition and Stampede, in Calgary, Alberta. This cartoon by Tom Innes, entitled "One of Calgary's briefcase-carrying cowboys," appeared in the July 16, 1983 issue of the Calgary Herald.*

These are almost caricatures with which I have taken some poetic license, but the point I am making is that there is a great gap between the view Albertans have of themselves and the one others have of them. There are reasons for the cowboy image that I have alluded to already—Calgary turns itself into a replica of the fictional Wild West for ten days every year and this image is extended to take in the entire province for the rest of the year. However, "cowboy" is also used in a derogatory sense to describe someone who acts without thinking and has fallen on his head too often. It is in this latter sense that the moniker is resented.

Assumptions that Albertans are selfish are not surprising as the provincial government often complains about the amount the province contributes to Confederation. The cost/benefit analysis which is an

I

ongoing exercise is then amplified by the media and by groups that are interested in distancing Alberta from Ottawa. As the general public is subjected to this steady drip of misinformation, some people have come to resent Alberta's wealth being sent outside the province. It can be labelled "misinformation" because the message from many opinion-makers in the province implies that equalization payments to have-not provinces come directly from provincial coffers—i.e., that the Alberta government is required to dip into provincial revenues and send a cheque to Ottawa on a regular basis.

In fact, equalization payments are made out of federal general revenue collected across the country in the form of federal taxes. On the heels of the sponsorship scandal and coverage of cost overruns on the Firearms Registry, to name just two recent examples, the provincial government has almost fostered discontent, encouraging Albertans to question the wisdom of sending revenue to Ottawa where it is wasted. Despite the Klein government's efforts, as mentioned earlier, the vast majority of Albertans (78%) support equalization payments as do Canadians in other provinces. The desire to share their wealth, even though they think that it is provincial revenue that is being sent to Ottawa, demonstrates that Albertans do not share the rather mean-spirited sentiments sometimes expressed on their behalf. This piece of information might come as a surprise to people who listen to complaints about Alberta's wealth being siphoned off and assume it causes widespread resentment. Another piece of information that is better known casts the province in an unfavourable light.

## Anti-Semitism

Many people believe that anti-Semitism lurks in the province, and that impression is grounded in events in the past. There was a definite anti-Semitic strand in Social Credit which fuels the perception that Albertans are Holocaust deniers. Social Credit's founder, Major Douglas, had strong views on the "Jewish cabal" that controlled finance, firmly believing that there was a Communist-Jewish conspiracy to control the world. In a letter to Adolf Hitler he referred to "the Jew" as "a parasite upon, and a corruption of every civilization in which he has obtained power" (Barr, 1974: 128). By the early 1940s, according to Alvin Finkel, he added Nazis to the list of conspirators, claiming that

World War II was a sham, part of a plot by Jews, Nazis, Communists, Socialists and financiers to enslave the world:

> It was a mad enough theory but it found a welcome reception among his Alberta followers, including Aberhart and his successor, Ernest Manning. Neither Aberhart nor Manning appears to have subscribed to Douglas's notion that the conspiracy had an ethnic character, but both accepted the view that there was an international conspiracy to fool people into not adopting the social credit solution to their woes (1989: 82–83).

The Social Credit Board, which had drafted the unsuccessful legislation in 1937–38, found itself isolated and underemployed. In 1943 its members began to pick up on Douglas's conspiracy theories and weave them into the Board's publications. By 1947 the Social Credit Board had become an embarrassment, so Manning dissolved it.

Many Social Credit members, including MPs, openly engaged in "Jew baiting" and the *Canadian Social Crediter*, published by the national wing of the party, routinely carried anti-Semitic material. Manning pressured the national executive to fire its editor. However, as Finkel points out, while Social Credit no longer attacked Jews, under Manning "it continued to view the world in conspiratorial terms and to govern accordingly" (189: 106). The target became world communism and socialism.

Despite the official renunciation of anti-Semitism, many prominent Social Credit members broke away and remained loyal to Douglas. They continued to support his increasingly paranoid views. That these ideas live on in the minds of some Albertans was brought to the attention of the country in 1983. That was when a school teacher in Eckville, Jim Keegstra, was dismissed because he had been teaching the Jewish conspiracy theory as fact to his students for eight years. In 1985, after a sensational trial which provided Keegstra and his lawyer, Doug Christie, with a soap box, he was convicted of hate crimes. The former junior high school teacher came from a staunch Social Credit family and was a former student at the Calgary Prophetic Bible Institute. This is an unsavoury legacy from the Social Credit era which continues to taint the perception of this province.

It is only fair to point out that anti-Semitism was widespread until the Holocaust jolted the world. It was more blatant in Alberta because

SOURCE: GLENBOW ARCHIVES M-8000-1252
*Peter Lougheed takes aim at "bigotry"—in this case, anti-Semitism.*

of Social Credit's founder, although there is no evidence that Aberhart or Manning were anti-Semites. Our next task is to examine whether most Albertans are social conservatives.

## Social Conservatism

Alberta is believed to contain a disproportionate share of social conservatives within its borders. However, I think the jury is out on this characteristic. It is hardly surprising that Alberta, particularly southern Alberta, is frequently referred to as the "Bible Belt," as it is the home of a substantial number of Mormons who moved up from Utah starting in the mid-1880s. In addition, for 36 years Alberta Premiers preached to their flock on CFCN Radio.

William Aberhart was a school principal who moonlighted as a lay preacher and radio evangelist. He had been involved with different churches, but founded the Calgary Prophetic Bible Institute in the 1920s. His interpretations of the Bible got him into trouble with three of the Churches, but, undaunted, he moved to the Westbourne Baptist Church where his popularity soared. As a result, his Sunday lectures were moved to the Palace Theatre which had the capacity to accommodate 2,000 people. When CFCN, the most powerful radio station in Alberta at that time, began to broadcast these talks in 1925, the audience swelled considerably. Estimates are that the message reached half a million listeners, including audiences in Saskatchewan and the US. Apparently no one walking down the street in small-town Alberta would miss a word of what Aberhart said because every radio would be tuned in to CFCN—a broadcaster's dream scenario!

As already pointed out, Aberhart popularized social credit doctrine in his radio broadcasts. Even after he became Premier, he continued with these broadcasts and his critics accused him of using his "pulpit" to get his political message out. On Aberhart's death in 1943, Ernest Manning, his protégé and a senior minister in the government became Premier. Manning took over both the political reins as well as the religious mantle of his mentor. During his 25 years in office he continued to broadcast "Canada's Back to the Bible Hour" initiated by Aberhart in 1925.

Religious leaders were active in politics in other prairie provinces as well. It was an era during which theologians were becoming more critical of the status quo, denouncing social injustice and calling for government intervention. Tommy Douglas was a Baptist minister before being elected in Saskatchewan and in Manitoba; J.S. Woodsworth, who was elected to the House of Commons, was a former Methodist minister. He abandoned his church when he came to the conclusion that it seemed more concerned with society's more fortunate members and was not doing enough for the needy. The title of Richard Allen's article "The Social Gospel as the Religion of the Agrarian Revolt," underscores the interweaving of politics and religion on the Prairies and parts of Ontario. Allen points out that leaders of Grain Growers organizations "were often churchmen of note or even clergy." In addition farmers' associations were often staffed by people with theological training or even men of the cloth (1985: 440).

What is unusual about the Alberta case is the unbroken 36-year period during which a sitting Premier combined political and religious duties. Given this background, it is not surprising that Alberta is still viewed as the "Bible belt" and a natural home for social conservatives. When the Reform Party was founded by Preston Manning, the son of Alberta's long-time Premier and a deeply religious man himself, the party no doubt attracted many whose values could be described as social conservative. This tendency was reinforced by the ascension of Stockwell Day to the leadership of the Canadian Alliance.

When Stephen Harper became the leader of the Alliance and then the Conservative Party, he gave the impression that he was a fiscal rather than a social conservative. However, his strong defense of the traditional definition of marriage during the same-sex marriage debate suggests his conservatism runs much deeper. More importantly, because Alberta is a Conservative stronghold, it reinforces the belief that Albertans overwhelmingly share everything the party stands for.

There is a common view that on issues such as abortion, gay rights and gun control, Albertans consistently have attitudes that differ significantly from the other provinces. The first two provide evidence of social conservative values and the third has been included to see if Alberta has a strong gun culture, making it more like the US. However, I would submit that the evidence is not clear-cut. Alberta is often singled out for attention when polling figures are reported and other "outliers" escape notice. For example, when wading through numerous polls, I came across comments like "of course, in Alberta, support was the lowest..." (sometimes it was the highest on opposition to something like abortion). This typecasting is frustrating because it is as if Alberta is the class clown of Confederation, incapable of behaviour that deviates from its prescribed role. The data shows that the other two prairie provinces are often closely aligned with Alberta, and in some cases their responses are more socially conservative. I should point out that results for the three prairie provinces are most often lumped together, so it is difficult to get a fix on attitudes in Alberta alone.

The following discussion will shed some light on attitudes on three controversial issues, but we have to bear in mind that surveys are only snapshots. Anyone who designs questionnaires for polling firms knows that it is possible to elicit the response you are looking for by wording the preamble in a particular way or by asking a leading question. It can also be structured in such a way that it precludes undesirable responses. The timing of a poll also influences the results: support for capital punishment would spike if a survey was conducted days after a child was molested and murdered. The size of the sample also affects its reliability. That is why polling numbers must be interpreted with caution. The most reliable data come from polls that are replicated year after year, but this is not the usual practice.

The three topics selected for investigation are emotionally charged, and it would be fair to say that they polarize the Canadian population. Let us look first at abortion. There is no question that abortion is a deeply divisive issue and the polls bear this out. Over the years, several organizations have commissioned polls to tap the public's attitudes on this matter. I am focusing on some questions in Leger Marketing's wide-ranging surveys for Alberta Pro-Life. These were done in three successive years (2001 through 2003), asked similar questions, and Alberta's results are reported separately—Manitoba and Saskatchewan are combined as the "Prairies." I have deliberately chosen a pro-life organization's data as it would, if anything, want to exaggerate opposition to abortion. It is also a set of findings that is frequently and approvingly cited by opponents of abortion. I have selected responses to questions that I feel go to the core of the issue. Unfortunately, Leger Marketing did not ask identical questions in each year, adding new ones and dropping others.

In 2001, they asked directly whether respondents favoured abortion, but this question was not repeated. In Alberta 39% of the sample answered in the affirmative, compared with 31% of those in Saskatchewan and Manitoba. The national figure is 47%. Support was highest in BC and Quebec, but what is interesting is that the number of respondents in the Atlantic region who support abortion, at 36%, was lower than in Alberta. Admittedly, this is only one poll but it does suggest that when the numerous others collapse all three prairie provinces, it is quite possible that Albertans are, at least slightly, out of step with their prairie cousins. In this case the gap is 8%.

Unfortunately, the direct question about support for abortion was not repeated in the following two years, so we have to try and get equivalent information from the questions that were posed. In 2002, respondents were asked at what point in human development they felt the law should protect human life, and the first choice was at conception.[3] Let us assume that those who would like to see the fetus protected at conception would also believe that is when life begins. We could then assume that they would oppose abortion because it would constitute taking a life. In 2002, 38% of Albertans chose conception, compared with 44% for the Prairies and 37% for the whole country. Interestingly, the corresponding figure for Atlantic Canadian respondents was 47%.

Getting a clear picture is difficult because there's a plethora of surveys, some asking when life begins, whether abortions should be publicly funded, and whether parents should be informed before abortions are performed on under-age children. Questions on abortion that are combined with views about the taxpayer having to foot the bill yield different results.[4]

Another way to gauge support for abortion would be to look at the actual numbers of abortions done. If a province is socially conservative one would assume that fewer abortions would be performed than in provinces with greater support.

In a 2001 Statistics Canada report on rates of therapeutic abortions per 1,000 women of child-bearing age, the rate for Alberta is just over 15, for Ontario just under 15. The corresponding figure for Saskatchewan is 9, for Manitoba 14, and for Canada as whole it is 16. The figures for 2000 were very similar. Statistics Canada reported in 2002 that the abortion rate decreased for most provinces, but in others, including Alberta, it increased slightly. The numbers seem to indicate that despite what the views of Albertans may be, their behaviour is very similar to their counterparts in Ontario, which is certainly not regarded as socially conservative. Once again, Saskatchewan is different.

Abortion continues to be a controversial issue across the country, but there is much more complexity and a good deal of obfuscation when figures are bandied about. Nevertheless, after wading through a great deal of data, it appears that Alberta's position at the top of the social conservative scale on this issue can be contested.

With respect to same-sex marriages, Albertans are polarized on this

---

3. The other alternatives were: at 3 months of pregnancy, at 6 months, or at birth.
4. A Leger poll in 2002 found 54% of Albertans favoured publicly-funded abortions only in an emergency. The corresponding national figure was 51%.

SOURCE: ARTIZANS.COM

*Ralph Klein sawing off a branch of the "Family Tree" (cartoon first appeared in the Edmonton Journal).*

issue like their counterparts in the rest of Canada. In 2001, Leger Marketing did a survey which had some interesting findings. They asked a series of questions about homosexuals: e.g. are they the same as everyone else? (63% of Albertans said they were); should they have the same rights as everyone else? (72% of Albertans said they should). Another asked whether we should grant them legal rights for same-sex marriages (among other things) and in this case 55% of Albertans agreed. Subsequent polls found very different attitudes and this is probably accounted for by two factors: first, in the Leger survey there is a lead-up to the question about same-sex marriage instead of it being posed in isolation; second, it is couched in terms of rights rather than morality.

A poll conducted by the Centre for Research and Information on Canada in 2003 found national support at 48% for same sex marriages and 47% against. Pollsters have been tracking these figures for several years and national support has climbed from 49% in 1996 to 54% in 2004. In Alberta, support for same-sex marriage dropped from 43% in

1999 to 37% in an Environics poll in 2004. In some polls which combine Saskatchewan and Manitoba, it was found that they have the lowest support for same-sex marriage, 8% lower than Alberta. When asked whether same-sex marriage is wrong and should never be legalized only 28% of Albertans (a tie with Quebecers) agreed, compared with 41% in the other prairie provinces. What has clouded the issue recently is that there is more opposition to changing the traditional definition of marriage to include couples of the same sex.

In Alberta, attitudes towards same-sex marriage have in all likelihood been affected by the Klein government's vigourous campaign against it. For a while there was some suggestion that the Notwithstanding Clause would be invoked to prevent such marriages in the province. However, the province has since backed off and recognized that there is little it can do to erect a firewall to prevent same-sex marriages within provincial borders.

As the debate on global warming demonstrates, Ralph Klein is able to shift public opinion significantly when he launches an attack on some federal policy.

In many countries including Canada, more stringent rules on gun ownership are triggered by tragic events that prompt public demands for action. In Canada it was the massacre of 14 young women in Montreal in 1989. In Britain, the impetus came from the murder of 16 school children and their teacher in Dunblane, Scotland in 1996. Also in 1996, when 35 people were killed in Tasmania, the Australian government felt stricter legislation was required. In all three countries, a horrified public put pressure on their governments to prevent a recurrence by introducing strict controls on ownership of weapons.

Gun control is not as divisive as the other two issues dealt with above. Until recently, there has consistently been majority support for gun control in every province, including Alberta. The Alberta Minister of Justice admitted that his government's own polls showed that a majority of Albertans were in favour of Bill C-68 which became The Firearms Act. Nevertheless, he appeared before the Standing Committee on Justice to register the provincial government's opposition to it.

An Environics poll in 2001 found that 77% of Canadians and 60% of Albertans were in favour of gun control legislation. In Manitoba (58%) and Saskatchewan (59%), the figure was slightly lower. National support slipped somewhat to 74% in 2003 and in Alberta there was a six-point decrease to 54%. However, Saskatchewan was the only province in which a majority, albeit a miniscule one, does not support gun control: by 2003 only 49% of those surveyed still supported the legislation. Manitoba was the only province in the country where support increased, going up to 62%. The same poll found that support for the Firearms Registry in all four western provinces is less than 50%. It is lowest (35%) in Saskatchewan and Alberta (38%).

Declining support for gun control measures in Alberta can be explained in part by the fact that the Alberta government challenged the constitutionality of Ottawa's legislation in 1998. It was joined by Ontario, Saskatchewan, Manitoba, New Brunswick, Nova Scotia and the two Territories in its challenge. The case was brought to the courts despite the fact that majorities in all the provinces supported gun control legislation. The case made it all the way to the Supreme Court where it was ruled that Ottawa has the constitutional right to pass such legislation. One may well ask whose interests governments in these provinces were representing when they embarked on the costly legal challenge.

The legislation itself was just the first hurdle: regulations had to be drafted, and the task proved lengthy due to the numerous roadblocks erected by opponents. The gun registry, which has cost far more than anticipated, has become a lightning rod so that it is now difficult to assess whether declining support for gun control is a result of cost overruns or whether Canadians have changed their minds about controlling guns in modern society. The amount of money spent on fighting the legislation right up to the Supreme Court and the cost of non-cooperation by some provincial governments on the gun registry adds up to a considerable sum.

There is no consensus on the three "hot button" issues discussed above. Canadians are split and Alberta has a reputation for being the most opposed to abortion, same-sex marriages and gun control. Yet, in polls from which one can compare Alberta with the Prairies it is apparent that the figures are close or they show that Alberta cannot be labelled the social conservative capital of Canada. Perhaps Alberta attracts a great deal of negative attention because the Alberta government is often at the forefront, framing the issue in regional terms to tap into the reservoir of western alienation that lurks below the surface. The enthusiasm with which Albertans have embraced video lottery terminals and privatized liquor stores suggests that their social conservative credentials are a little suspect.

What about the right-wing reputation Albertans have? This will be dealt with more fully in the next chapter. For the moment it will be sufficient to point out that Ralph Klein's attack on the deficit by cutting spending on programs like health care and education and by downsizing the civil service generated a great deal of interest within Canada and in the US. Other jurisdictions which were in similar circumstances wanted to see how much pain Albertans could withstand. However, since the government has started posting surpluses, spending has increased and critics are now accusing the Premier of having lost his way. As we shall see in Chapter 5, other Alberta governments have not *behaved* in a manner that can be labeled "right-wing."

The issue of one-party dominance is also considered a distinctive feature of the province. Alberta's electoral history causes a great deal of comment for two reasons: first because two "third" parties governed the province for half a century and because turnover does not take place often. However, one-party dominance is not unique to the province. The Liberals held office in Quebec between 1897 and 1936 and then the Union Nationale was in power for almost a quarter-century. The Conservatives had an unbroken 42-year reign in Ontario, so Alberta is in good company. What is different about Alberta is that no party that has been swept out of office has been re-elected. The UFA did not contest elections after its defeat and the Social Credit, which never recovered from its defeat at the hands of the Conservatives, has virtually disappeared from the radar screen. That means only the Liberals have not made a comeback.

With "third" parties in government for so long, both the traditional parties competed against each other as well as the governing party. However, they had even more competition: as MLAs in Calgary and Edmonton were elected on the basis of proportional representation, a number of Independents contested the election and small parties ran candidates. These Independents and minor party candidates won seats, often six or seven, during this period. These siphoned off votes from the Liberals and Conservatives, preventing either from mounting a serious challenge to the government.

According to the Elections Alberta website, an average of 8 parties has contested elections in Alberta since 1905, and even though their chances of success have decreased since the province reverted to the first-past-the post system with single-member constituencies, the number of parties is sometimes in double digits. In the last provincial election there were 10 parties on the ballot in some constituencies. The electoral system utilized between 1921 and 1959 might partly explain why one strong opposition party did not emerge as an alternative to the government of the day.

When Alberta is said to have stampedes rather than elections, the allusion is to the number of seats won by the governing party. However, the gap between seat and vote percentage is wide, often over 30%. According to the Elections Alberta website, the highest percentage of the vote ever obtained by the governing party was 63%, which the Lougheed Conservatives received in the 1982 election. However, they received 92% of the seats. The average percentage of the vote received by the winning party since 1905 is right on 50%, not exactly a stampede towards a single party.

If we look at the federal level, although the Conservatives almost swept the province in the 2004 federal election, they did so with 60% of the vote. Here is another piece of evidence that Albertans are not all of one mind. Nevertheless, the myth continues to be perpetuated.

As mentioned above, when Albertans step out of character their actions are ignored. Mark Lisac points to coverage of demonstrations held across the country in March 2003 against the Iraq war to illustrate bias. The media neglected to note that the number of demonstrators (estimates range between 12,000 and 18,000) in Edmonton was the second largest in the country and was perhaps the largest demonstration in Alberta history (2003: 13). He speculates that this was not picked up by the national media because it did not fit the "template." Lisac argues: "Alberta is often not an outlier in the spectrum of Canadian public opinion despite frequent expressions of regionalism. It fits quite easily into that broad spectrum with only minor variations" (2003: 14).

The foregoing discussion suggests that there is reason to question some of the perceptions many people have of Alberta. The evidence is not conclusive, so we should not rush to judgement on a province that is often subjected to more scrutiny than any other. In addition, when the facts do no fit the pattern, they are sometimes ignored. Because of the province's history, the population is perhaps more susceptible to the views expressed by provincial elites when they are forming opinions. The process of opinion formation will be examined in detail in Chapter 6.

# 5

## Alberta Political Culture

The reputation that Albertans have developed over the years is becoming so entrenched that it is accepted uncritically in most circles. These views of Alberta's exceptionalism are based on slender evidence that ignores two key points: first, the very close bonds that linked Alberta to its two prairie cousins and second, elements in its early history which provide a very different picture of the province. As we have just seen, the contemporary view is also misleading. Perhaps the strongest impression people have of Alberta's distinctiveness is that it is a very American province, so it might be best to address this before examining the evidence on the province's political culture.

### The American Question

There are frequent references to the fact that Alberta is the most American of Canadian provinces, and Calgary the most American city. Depending on the source, the statement could be hurled as an insult, meaning a Texas North with all the negative connotations that implies, or as a compliment invoking qualities like individualism, self-reliance and risk-taking.

It would be useful to try and establish whether or not these American values permeate this province and therefore distinguish it from the rest of the country. The goal is to establish the veracity of this claim and not to imply that the American influence is good or bad. What is important is the motivation underlying this assertion: within the province it is part of the narrative that describes Albertans as self-reliant individualists who are different from (perhaps superior to?) other Canadians and is designed to mobilize the provincial population. Outside Alberta it appeals to stereotypical views which feed the misconceptions mentioned in the previous chapter.

Most often such claims are made in the media, and I have already mentioned (in a footnote in Chapter 4) the column by Barbara Yaffe which is a good example of the "genre." Fred Stenson, writing in *Alberta Views* magazine deals with this question in a light-hearted but competent manner (2002: 15). He critiques an article in the *National Post* which trots out all the hoary chestnuts regarding the concentration of American ranchers and cowboys, workers in the oil and gas industry all located in Calgary, and punctures the myths. Stenson also mentions the proverbial Ontarian who moves to the city and is amazed at how "normal" Calgarians are. In a video link-up between one of my classes and a class at an Ontario University, a student confessed that when he visited Calgary he was surprised that the downtown "had tall buildings and all"—the Calgary Stampede has done such a superlative job that visitors expect the city to look like the set of a Western movie!

There is no question that Alberta is home to tens of thousands of Americans who work primarily in the oil and gas industry. A figure of 80,000 for Calgary alone is quoted in the article by Stenson, but the City of Calgary website puts it at 50,000. These numbers are the basis of the contention that Calgary is an American city. Stenson wonders why Toronto, with 500,000 people of Italian descent, is not considered an Italian city (2002: 10).

There is also academic material dealing with the American influence on Alberta which makes a similar argument about the province as a whole. In an article on settlement patterns on the Prairies, political scientist Nelson Wiseman (1992) compares the ethnic backgrounds of settlers who peopled the three provinces. There are numerous others who focus on the American influence, but for the sake of simplicity I am using Wiseman's analysis, as it is representative of the views of many others who single out the Alberta experience. He refers to four groups: the first two were migrants from Canada (Anglo-Saxon Ontarians) and a new British group (urban and working class). The third and fourth groups were American (from the Great Plains states) and other immigrants (from Central and Eastern Europe). Transplanted Ontarians were influential and privileged wherever they went and were prominent in the community. In fact, historians feel that Manitoba was the battleground which determined which vision of Canada prevailed: Quebec's or Ontario's. Ontario won. The influence of Ontarians was dominant in all three provinces until at least 1921 according to Wiseman: "During World War I, for example, all three provincial Premiers, their ministers of agriculture, and a majority of MLAs were Ontarians" (1992: 645).

Wiseman places Alberta in a separate category, arguing that Americans flowed into southern Alberta bringing with them ideas and values from the American plains states. Despite the fact that there were equal numbers of Americans and Britons in Alberta in the 1920s, the former were more numerous in rural areas where they had disproportionate electoral clout. As Wiseman describes it, what the Americans brought

> was a radical "populist" liberalism that stressed the individual rather than the community or the state as a tory or socialist would. This wave's greatest impact was in rural Alberta, the continent's last agricultural frontier (1992: 642).

This is an accurate summation, but his contention is that the ideological strain carried by the Americans was liberal is open to question. (The reader will recall that Canadian political culture is believed to be predominantly liberal but with tory and socialist strands woven into the ideological mix.)

Let us first deal with the numerical strength of American settlers, as estimates vary widely and different figures are quoted for the same time period. In a table on the ethnic composition of the Prairies and Ontario, Roger Gibbins lists 14 ethnic groups, but there is no category for Americans. Gibbins explains that the figures are derived from the Canadian census which "does not recognize the United States as a point of ethnic origin and thus the isolation of Americans within census data is difficult at some times and impossible at others" (1980: 21). In refuting the argument that the CCF's failure in Alberta was due to the large number of Americans in the province, Palmer and Palmer point out that there was a negligible difference between Saskatchewan and Alberta with respect to the size of the American population in the 1930s (1990: 277). Depending on the source of the figures then (and Wiseman's essay does not mention his), it is prudent to view them with caution.

The thrust of Wiseman's argument is that with the huge influx of Americans came ideas and values that were absorbed by Albertans. One could argue that the actual numbers are not that important because even a small group can be very influential. This is certainly true of individuals like Henry Wise Wood who came from Missouri. Wood was in his mid-40s when he came to Canada and had observed populist movements in the US. As president of the UFA his views were authoritative and his reluctance to plunge the organization into direct political action was instrumental in delaying that move until 1919.

Others have noted the influence of American populism (Harrison, 2000; Laycock, 1990) in Alberta, but Wiseman's argument that the variant adopted in Alberta stressed the individual rather than the group, is contestable. As previously noted, American populist ideas did influence Wood, and therefore the UFA, because the terminology used by Wood was almost identical to that employed by the Populist/People's Party in the US. It represented the agrarian populism that gained strength in the 1890s at the time Wood was still in Missouri.

In the decades after the Civil War when industrialization accelerated and agriculture became more mechanized and commercialized, many American farmers lost their farms. Their criticism of the growth of economic oppression as well as the great gap between the rich and the poor was radical enough to alarm the wealthy. The Great Plains states were in a ferment, and some argue that the agrarian revolt was "the largest democratic mass movement in America … its most vivid demonstration of what authentic political life can be (Epp, 2002: 2). At the time it was believed that the introduction of direct legislation (initiatives and referenda) would empower wage workers and destroy the plutocrats. "In particular, the initiative would be the means by which the people would ensure the government served 'the mass of the people' rather than 'the greed of corporate wealth'" (Ellis, 2002: 33). Hofstadter (n.d.) argues that the farming community believed that the major parties were the cause of their problems and only a new party that was independent of corporate influence could represent their interests. These concerns were very similar to those expressed by the prairie farming community, and especially the farmers in Alberta. The traditional old-line parties were labelled as tools of corporate interests in Central Canada, and this reinforced non-partisan sentiment in the province.

It would be hard to argue that Wood's views exemplify right-wing populism as Wiseman seems to suggest. As we will see below, it was quite the opposite. Populist movements in Canada can be categorized as Left- or Right-populism according to John Richards. He argues that the former sprang from cooperative movements in rural areas that involved alliances between farmers and labour and critiqued corporate capitalism. The target of Right-populists is often banks which control the money supply (quoted in Harrison, 2000: 109). The latter sounds like Social Credit, but as we shall see, it was not that straightforward.

The populist nature of Alberta is, I feel, somewhat overstated, and if one examines the "populist" parties like the UFA and Social Credit, it might give one pause. The way in which average Albertans understand it, populism represents power to the people, i.e. plain folks rather than elites. According to Harrison (2000), the defining characteristics of all strands of populism are that they are mass political movements based on a direct relationship between leaders and followers. They also mobilize around important cultural symbols and a group's sense of threat which is an external one. Laycock (1990) identifies the desire to eliminate power relationships that privilege elites as a characteristic of populism. Reform Party leader Preston Manning's oft-repeated phrase "the common sense of the common people" taps into this vein to convey a message to the membership. The message is that the views of "ordinary folk" are sensible and welcome in the party. Both the UFA and Social Credit had a mass membership and respected leaders. There was the external threat (Ottawa) and the leaders were accessible, but the test is how the populist nature of the two parties manifested itself. Of the two, the UFA provides a better example of rank-and-file participation.

What needs to be established is whether populism can be detected in some form such as direct democracy or through avenues for genuine input from the grassroots. The popularity of the Reform Party in the early 1990s demonstrated that direct democracy still resonates in Alberta. Based on the fact that Albertans still seem to prefer non-partisanship and favour such mechanisms as initiative, referendum and recall, that would locate them in the camp of American populists from the Midwest. But to what extent were these devices operationalized?

The UFA was very democratic in its internal structure even before it entered politics, but once the UFA government dispensed with delegate democracy, the input of members into political decision-making was limited. Referring to grassroots activity in rural Alberta in the 1920s and early 1930s, Roger Epp observes that in meeting places across the province, people were engaged in political debate. They listened to speakers brought in by the UFA and as a result "rural communities were intensely political places" (2002). When the Depression took hold it affected everyone in close-knit rural Alberta, so interest in finding solutions was intense. While the UFA, which one should not forget was also an association of farmers, provided a forum for ideas to be explored, its behaviour as a political party was remarkably like that of a conventional party. Premier Brownlee's caution eventually drove UFA supporters into the arms of Social Credit because his government refused to undertake radical action. Brownlee cannot be faulted for not succumbing to pressure because, as Aberhart's experience demonstrated, the remedies being demanded were clearly unconstitutional.

The demands of UFA supporters was characteristic of populists: they were eager for an assault on the corporate and political forces ranged against them, caring little for constitutional niceties or the fate of their credit ratings in the future. However, the UFA leadership was not interested in implementing the revolutionary populist ideas espoused by its followers. This is why I would argue that after Brownlee took over, the populist nature of the UFA government is in some doubt.

We have already seen that despite Wood's strongly held views about the farmers entering the political arena as an occupational group, this did not eventuate when they actually gained power. I am not questioning Wood's sincerity: it is possible that having formed the government, the farmers discovered that "group government" was not feasible. The notion of delegate democracy met a similar fate, and probably for the same reason. UFA MLAs were political neophytes and their critics watched gleefully as they made mistakes in their first term.

At the outset MLAs did not even understand the mechanics of how a bill goes through three readings before it becomes law. The Speaker had to explain the process when backbenchers thought they could make amendments even after the third reading. It would be so easy to laugh at these anecdotes, but I suspect, despite the coaching new legislators receive today, there are many rookies for whom the Alberta legislature or the House of Commons is a bewildering place. The learning curve was very steep for the UFA. After discovering the constraints within which a legislature in a parliamentary system must operate, the UFA buckled down and operated as parties must within such a system.

When Aberhart was popularizing Social Credit there were thousands of Albertans involved in study groups to learn about, and then to teach, Social Credit. He himself taught the first group of 30 students at the Calgary Prophetic Bible Institute and this group then fanned out, teaching other small groups. The study groups numbered about 1,600 on the eve of the 1935 election. This certainly was a grassroots effort and is often likened to a prairie fire. One can accept that Social Credit was a mass movement at this point in its evolution, as it meets Harrison's criteria for a populist party. However, this was very short-lived.

Prior to the election, Social Credit's supporters were actively participating in an exercise in political education and mobilization, and the numbers are impressive. However, there are two points that need to be made on the Social Credit phenomenon: first, the main function of the numerous study groups was mainly to broadcast a message. They had a script for explaining Social Credit and a fistful of pamphlets written by Aberhart to help them in their task. Second, having completed their job of spreading the word, this army of mobilized Albertans was not invited to participate after Social Credit won the election. Although ready to answer the call, they were told by Aberhart that implementation of Social Credit would be left to the experts. Once again, the populist flame was doused. Social Credit had annual conventions and these provided opportunities for input. Many resolutions were passed, but met the same fate as resolutions at party conventions today. A number of Aberhart's followers remained very active in the religious end of the movement and it is sometimes difficult to separate the religious from the political activities.

The Conservative Party does not meet the necessary criteria to be defined as a populist party, nor has it claimed to be one. Although Peter Lougheed was a strong and respected leader, Albertans did not have a direct relationship with him or his successor, Don Getty. However, Ralph

Klein has been described as a populist, someone with whom the little guy can identify. His legendary visits to the humble St. Louis hotel in Calgary while he was mayor cemented his reputation as a man of the people.

Klein's beginnings are humble, so his claim to be just an ordinary guy strikes a chord with Martha and Henry, the typical Alberta couple often used to exemplify "severely normal Albertans." (Jean Chrétien, the "Little Guy from Shawinigan," exploited his humble beginnings and some people describe him as a populist.) Are humble beginnings a sufficient qualification, or should this go hand-in-hand with measures to improve the lot of average people? By targeting expenditures on social programs during the deficit reduction campaign, one could argue Ralph Klein did the opposite.

The government did embark on numerous consultative exercises to tap into public sentiment, providing an opportunity for public participation. There were roundtables, summits, surveys and presumably internal polling. The problem was that these were carefully orchestrated events often with handpicked participants, who, it appeared, were intended to sprinkle holy water on what the government wanted to do. Interestingly, the chosen few sometimes confounded the government by making unexpected recommendations.

Although Alberta elected its first populist party in 1921, ironically it was the Liberals in 1913 that actually delivered populist legislation, albeit at the behest of the UFA. (Recall was briefly available in the 1930s.) The legislation that introduced initiatives and referendums was in place for 46 years and it was used only once. This casts some doubt on the populist credentials of the people of this province in the post-UFA era.

It would be fair to say that as far as populism goes, despite a strong rhetorical commitment to it, Albertans have not behaved like populists for over seven decades. As far as the parties are concerned, the UFA did at least try to practise delegate democracy after it was elected. With respect to Social Credit, the evidence is not clear cut. There was grassroots involvement before the election victory, but after that the experts took over. Macpherson (1964) has labeled this plebiscitarian democracy and Laycock (1990) refers to it as plebiscitarian populism, but both fell well short of redefining democratic processes. Populist parties are a particular type of mass party and have met the same fate as such parties.

Political scientists categorize parties according to their origins, organizational structure and so on. Unlike cadre parties which form within the legislature when groups of like-minded individuals come together to form a party, mass parties originate outside the legislature. The membership is large and has a significant degree of influence over elected members—at least in theory. The Labour Party in Britain and the NDP and social democratic parties in Europe are examples of mass parties. Unfortunately, for all their good intentions, these parties inevitably yield to control by a small group. Almost a century ago, Roberto Michels observed that social democratic parties in Europe succumbed to the "iron law of oligarchy." In other words, no matter how democratic their ideology and their origins, they were eventually controlled by a clique in the legislature or on the party executive (cited in Van Loon and Whittington, 1987: 310).

This is hardly surprising, as it is difficult to sustain interest at a high level to keep the population sufficiently aroused. Conditions following World War I and during the Depression were desperate for many people, so the ground was fertile for mobilization of the population. When conditions reach normalcy, most people just want to get on with their lives.

Arguably, political parties have utilized the populist discourse to such good effect that it is accepted by many scholars, the media and the general public. The UFA wanted to avoid operating like a traditional party, but in the end it had to conform. Since then there has been no serious attempt to implement direct democracy except for Social Credit's short-lived Recall Act. The preceding discussion demonstrates that the frequent references to populist tendencies in Alberta are not supported by the evidence. Agrarian discontent on both sides of the border was prompted by similar problems and elicited a similar response as farmers sought greater input into decisions affecting their lives. I would argue that the American strain that found its way to Alberta was left-wing populism.

If not populists in the right-wing American mould, then what are Albertans? Are they unique or do they share characteristics at least with their prairie cousins?

## The Prairie Connection
The Canadian Prairies could have used Frederick Jackson Turner. He

was a historian at the University of Wisconsin in 1893 when he put the American West on the map. Turner is the author of the famous (or infamous to some) Frontier Thesis which provoked much scholarly debate and captured the popular imagination. His thesis was a reaction to the US Census of 1890 which reported that the frontier had ceased to exist —i.e., there was no more free land for settlers.

Turner argued that the frontier, a shifting one, was the cradle of American democracy, the place where rugged individualism, resourcefulness and initiative were born as people confronted the wilderness. He rejected the idea that democracy was the product of the European heritage and dismissed the contributions of such events as the anti-slavery movement and the Civil War and other important American milestones (Limerick, 1995: 699). These controversial views were at first ignored, then embraced and then criticized, but what is interesting is that as a result of the furore, the history of the West began to creep into the eastern curriculum. The West began to be noticed and then glorified in novels, movies and western music.

What if we had a Canadian Turner to celebrate the achievements of pioneer communities on the Canadian Prairies? Would the sense of alienation ever have developed? One could fantasize for hours on how different the country might be if a flattering narrative was told about the opening up of the Canadian West. I use the word "flattering" advisedly because Turner's critics (Limerick, 1995) have pointed out that there was a dark underside to westward expansion which is ignored by him. It was not such a happy experience for American Indians, nor was the rough justice meted out on the frontier particularly edifying. Whether the American frontier was built by rugged individualists has also been questioned because the cooperative aspects of the agricultural frontier have been ignored. The Frontier Thesis was appealing to people in the West precisely because it portrayed them in such a favourable light. There is much that can be fashioned from the off-cuts of history, and some of that work has begun, but the Prairies have not yet been placed on the cutting edge of Canadian democracy. The Canadian Prairies have not captured the popular imagination, but their early history contains the seeds of an epic drama.

Bound together by the imperatives of the wheat economy, people on the Prairies were shaped by the challenges they faced and were unified by them. Alberta is now very affluent; it has changed so dramatically in a century that it often seems that Albertans do not want to acknowledge their less affluent cousins. The family resemblance was much stronger a century ago.

In the 21st century we have iPods, we have e-mail to communicate instantly and can travel across the globe in hours. It is therefore almost impossible to imagine the physical isolation of the prairie frontier when settlers first arrived. The vast, empty, and bitingly cold plains attracted immigrants from all over Europe as well as other parts of North America. In a frenzy of false advertising, the federal government depicted the Prairies as a sort of Shangri-La where the climate was healthful and the harvest bountiful. Immigrants flocked here believing they were entering a paradise where they would be masters of their own destinies. The reality was of course, slightly different and settlers had to cope with harsh climatic conditions, devise ways to farm virgin soil and do much of it alone. They discovered very quickly that their fate lay in distant hands.

Prairie pioneers experienced an alienation on three levels: political, economic, and intellectual, and each had consequences (Barr, 1974: 14–15). At the time of settlement new Canadians did not receive a citizenship kit which explained how the political system worked, nor were they informed about the nature of the existing party system. Consequently, even immigrants who had come from Britain or the US were unfamiliar with Canadian political parties. In fact, some settlers had no experience at all with democratic forms of government. Their experiences led them to the conclusion that the two parties were tools of Central Canadian interests, so people on the Prairies invented their own political instruments.

In the economic realm, the strong feeling that the entire region was in a position of economic subservience to Central Canada resulted in experimentation of a different kind. The farming community set up structures such as the UFA and its counterparts in Saskatchewan and Manitoba to protect their economic interests. Wheat pools, another innovation, were co-operative, self-help organizations that were established in the 1920s. They were spawned by disillusionment with existing structures, structures which were seen to be exploiting the farming community.

Intellectual alienation meant that prairie residents were cut off from the intellectual currents of the day. Without access to radio or television there were no pundits to keep them abreast of current events and tell them what to think. Communication was slow and the highways we now take for granted did not exist. Their ideas were shaped by what they experienced every day, and later by the experiences of their American counterparts. The consequence was the emergence of a distinctive regional way of looking at and dealing with regional problems.

The various strands of alienation combined to become what is now known as "western alienation," a phenomenon that Gibbins defines as

> a *political ideology of regional discontent* ... [which] embodies a socially shared set of interrelated beliefs with some degree of cultural embodiment and intellectual articulation, with a recognized history and constituency, and with recognized spokesmen and carriers of the creed (1980: 169).

It has a long history and the components are transmitted from one generation to the next through the process of socialization. These beliefs revolve around a sense of regional neglect by Ottawa, and a feeling of "cultural estrangement from the Canadian heartland" (Gibbins, 1980: 169). Not surprisingly, what follows is the assumption that the region's interests, especially its economic interests, are subordinated to those of the central Canadian provinces.

The sense that the West, particularly the prairie provinces, is a colony of the Canadian heartland, is as old as the region itself. In the early years, the concerns related to agriculture—freight rates, tariffs and transportation policies—were pointed to as evidence of unfair treatment. There was also retention of ownership of natural resources on the Prairies until 1930, which provided tangible evidence of discriminatory treatment. The stage was thus set for the development of a regional consciousness, the political ideology of regional discontent.

There was a remarkable identity of interest in prairie communities when wheat was king. The entire population was either growing it, getting it to market or providing goods and services to those who were. In other circumstances, the polyglot nature of the population might have caused more friction than it did.[1] However, the weather, the price of

---

1. The culturally diverse population did not live in perfect harmony and I do not want to gloss over the difficulties faced by many immigrant groups who were picked on and

wheat, grain companies and financial institutions treated everyone alike. One searing bond that united the Prairies was the suffering of the 1930s. No region in Canada suffered more than the Prairies during the Depression. Per capita income dropped by a staggering 71% in Saskatchewan and 61% in Alberta. Manitoba was slightly better off as its economy was not so dependent on agriculture, but it too experienced a 49% decrease in per capita income. The situation changed dramatically after World War II when the structure of the economies of the Prairies diversified and the interests diverged. The identity of interest that had bound the region gradually dissolved.

## Alberta: Disconnected?

Up to the beginning of World War II, the Prairies were a region apart, but the common national project of fighting a war effected a change in the way Canadians everywhere saw the boundaries of their world. In the aftermath of the war, a sense of national pride and national purpose imbued the population, and Albertans too were infused with these sentiments. It was in this climate that the national government assembled the separate pieces of the welfare state. Public support for these measures was widespread and Albertans were no less supportive than their counterparts elsewhere. The Alberta population was not immune to larger currents of opinion that swept the country, but there were also internal developments that were changing the province.

The oil strike at Leduc transformed Alberta beyond recognition, virtually deleting from the collective memory what had gone before. It is, therefore, worth reminding readers that this province's early history was far from calm and conservative.

In their quest for fairness and a measure of control over their lives, the farming community came up with some fairly revolutionary ideas. The Non-Partisan League (NPL) which had its founding meeting in Calgary in 1917 declared that its objective was "the overthrow of party-ism and substitution of a business administration in the province, and government ownership and control of every feasible public utility"

---

ridiculed for their strange clothes, unfamiliar food and incomprehensible language. However, they proved to be resilient and were able to retain many of the customs and cuisine that enriches Canada today. It was not easy.

(quoted in Thomas, 1959: 178). The socialist flavour of the NPL is echoed in the previously mentioned Farmers' Platform endorsed by Alberta farmers, which, among other demands, called for railways and telecommunications networks to be publicly run.

Alberta's early radicalism is almost forgotten, overlaid by decades of stability and blunted by affluence. While the activism of the farming community is well known, relatively little is known about the labour movement. It might come as a surprise that Western members of national and international unions were considered more radical than their Eastern counterparts. Miners in the Crow's Nest area were particularly militant.[2] During and shortly after World War I, some unionists supported large industrial unions and a general strike and others visualized a workers' revolution. Western labour leaders led by the Socialist Party of Canada (SPC) organized a Western Labour Conference in Calgary to which unions from all the western provinces were invited. Friesen contends that the SPC leadership was surprised when the conference in March 1919 became "a revolutionary love-in":

> The delegates cheered radical speeches and roared their disapproval when voices of moderation were tentatively raised. They endorsed the principle of "proletarian dictatorship" as a means of translating capitalist private property into communal wealth, and they sent fraternal greetings to such groups as the Russian Bolsheviks... (1987: 36).

The leaders decided to hold a referendum on whether western workers should secede from the international craft unions and form One Big Union. It is almost impossible to imagine Alberta as a hotbed of revolutionaries, but in the winter of 1918–19 the situation was chaotic with the influenza epidemic raging and soldiers returning in their thousands to an uncertain future. In May 1919 approximately 25,000 workers in Winnipeg walked off the job, triggering the Winnipeg General Strike which lasted over a month. Coming on the heels of the Calgary meeting,

---

2. According to Palmer and Palmer (1990:155-56), mines in Alberta were among the most dangerous in the world. The disaster that triggered the Frank Slide in April 1903 took 70 lives but there were many others. The deadliest mine disaster in Canadian history occurred in Hillcrest, Alberta in June 1914. The death toll was 189. Between 1904 and 1963 the number of fatalities in Alberta mines was 1200 (*Alberta Views*, 2005: 98).

there was indeed fear that a Bolshevik revolution was in the making and a proletarian dictatorship was about to be established. Authorities dealt harshly with the strikers, imprisoning some for sedition. Violence erupted and two people were killed when police fired on a crowd that had overturned a streetcar.

Interestingly, even union leaders couched their grievances in regional terms. Masson and Blaikie comment that the International Workers of the World, which organized unskilled workers in coal mining areas in the province, "channeled pent-up western hostility toward the East's high protective tariffs and dominant financial interests" (1979: 272). The regional card was always available to be played when the occasion arose.

The Communist Party had support among immigrant miners in the 1920s, but during the Depression they made further inroads. Communists dominated farmers' and workers' organizations and, although they were led by British immigrants with experience in the British labour movement, Howard and Tamara Palmer (1990) point out that 95% were from Central and Eastern Europe. They were successful getting a communist elected as a Calgary alderman in 1938. As is often the case with radical organizations, affiliates of the Communist Party such as the Hungarian Mutual Benefit Federation provided insurance benefits, sports, and cultural activities to their members. Idealistic young Canadians joined because they felt the left had

> an explanation for the troubles plaguing our society... Most important of all, they had a program of action, based on unity of labour and farmers to compel government to take immediate remedial action ... it was the communists who led most struggles for jobs, for relief, against wage cuts (quoted in Palmer and Palmer, 1990: 249).

The relationship between farmers and labour was formalized when the Co-operative Commonwealth Federation (CCF) held its founding convention in Calgary in 1932, but they had cooperated informally for years. William Irvine, who was involved with the Non-Partisan League, was later a member of the UFA and was elected as a Progressive in 1921. He was also a founder of the CCF. The coalition of labour groups and farmer's organizations grew out of the realization that they had common grievances and interests which could be better addressed through cooperation. Despite holding the founding convention in Calgary, the CCF did not make the hoped-for breakthrough. Many people assume that the CCF's failure to do so in Alberta was because there is no market for social democratic ideas in the province, but this is not the case. It may have been partly because of its connection with the United Farmers of Alberta. Finkel argues that:

> [t]he socialist alternative was not rejected out-of-hand by Albertans in favour of Social Credit which in any case did not form a separate party until 1935. Rather the socialist alternative, the CCF, negated itself by tying its fate to two increasingly discredited organizations [the UFA and the Canadian Labour Party] instead of establishing itself as a new grass-roots party without ties to existing parties (1989: 25).

A key argument Finkel makes is that when Social Credit first came to power it was quite different from the party of the 1940s and beyond. Resolutions passed at Social Credit conventions closely resembled those passed at CCF conventions. He also points out that there were electoral alliances between Social Credit and the Communist Party at the local, provincial and federal levels (1989: 50).

In 1933 Aberhart wrote a pamphlet explaining his version of Social Credit. It was referred to as the "Yellow Pamphlet" for its colour. Aberhart got help from a friend, who was a Communist and in Elliott's view, changes proposed in the document were very radical: among other measures, it would require citizens with money in financial institutions to turn it over to the government in exchange for government bonds (1987:110–11). These left-wing views were reflected in the *Social Credit Chronicle*, published by Social Credit groups. In one issue, the editorial called on Alberta "to take the lead in showing the country that the people have broken away from the old yoke of the capitalistic system" (quoted in Finkel, 1989: 33).

Aberhart's view of the world was confusing and contradictory, but some of the measures his government implemented were certainly on the left side of the political spectrum. When Manning was minister of Trade and Industry, during Social Credit's first term, it was the job of his ministry to regulate commercial and industrial activity in the province. Some of the measures passed on his watch were described by the *Globe and Mail* as "a long step on the road to state socialism, to the regimentation of Canadian farmers and other primary producers" (quoted in

Finkel, 1989: 45). The target of this denunciation was the Provincial Marketing Board established in 1939 with wide-ranging powers. There were apparently few restrictions on its potential actions, as it could be involved in buying and selling of a huge swath of products and manufactures as a wholesaler, retailer, broker, factor or agent. It could engage in manufacturing, producing, processing, handling or distribution of merchandise or natural products (Finkel, 1989: 44–45). These sweeping powers were not exercised, but they illustrate how far the Social Credit government and Manning's ministry were prepared to intervene in the economy. He later admitted that he had learned the disadvantages of government getting involved in matters the private sector could handle better (Elliott: 2004: 163).

The rightward tilt began to manifest itself after Ernest Manning took over the helm, but, judging from the election results, whether it reflected a similar shift among rank and file members is not clear. The right turn was partly a tactical move to respond to the CCF's popularity towards the end of the war. Manning campaigned vigourously against the CCF in 1944 and what might have been a strategic decision initially became ingrained in Social Credit thereafter. He had reason to be concerned. At that time, the CCF was the most popular party in the country and this was true in Alberta as well. The party had won the Saskatchewan election shortly after the Alberta election was called.

The election result testifies to the popularity of the CCF in Alberta. It received half as many votes as Social Credit but received only two seats; Social Credit received 51 seats. The popular vote (i.e. the number of votes cast for a party) is a much more accurate reflection of public opinion than the seat count for each party. The discrepancy is partly an artefact of the electoral system.[3]

Because Manning believed that the socialists and communists were plotting to take over the world, he portrayed his party as a friend of business and developed a cordial relationship with the corporate sector. The new Premier had to set about presenting Social Credit as a more

---

3. As mentioned earlier, Alberta had a different electoral system between 1926 and 1959. In that period Calgary and Edmonton were multiple-member ridings using proportional representation. Alberta was one of the most extreme examples of rural over-representation.

moderate party to erase memories of Aberhart's intemperate language when he railed against banks and the corporate sector in Central Canada. This dovetailed neatly with the anti-socialist strategy. After the Leduc oil strike, Social Credit's earlier dalliance with communists and socialists was air-brushed from its history, but as revenues increased so did spending.

That the Manning government saw health and education at high priorities is evident from spending in these areas. According to the provincial public accounts, in the decade from 1958–68 his government spent generously on health and education, allocating 40% and 30% respectively to these two areas (Watkins, 1980: 189). Aberhart, being an educator, showed his strong commitment to education in his battle to retain its budget when every other area was cut back in the depths of the Depression. Albertans supported these priorities.

One would expect that people who pride themselves on their self-reliance and their ability to cope with whatever fate throws in their path would not seek government assistance or tolerate government interference in their lives. Libertarians would take this line of thinking to the extreme, preferring to go it alone at all costs. However, if one assumes that Albertans are a paler copy, supporting small government, resenting interference and expecting little help, then the people of this province have not played their assigned role. One would also expect the government of the day to play a minor role in society and in the economy.

Alberta has not had minimalist governments, and the size of its regulatory apparatus is a measure of such a government. The Alberta section of the Canadian Bar Association found in 1960 that the province had 123 boards and tribunals as opposed to 86 for the much larger and highly industrialized province of Ontario. These bodies presided over everything from film censorship and the pricing of milk to sterilizing of mental defectives (Barr, 1974: 134).

Manning said he believed in private enterprise and violently rejected "the slippery, slimy slopes of socialism," yet he supported a state-regulated society. Watkins states that he recommended that Ottawa set up a national financial commission with the same powers the socialists called for and adds,

> Manning would have taken away from the chartered banks the power to make economic decisions. The first step the socialist government in Britain took in 1945 was to

nationalize the Bank of England, using the same arguments
with the same intentions (Watkins, 1980: 147).

Politicians often say one thing and do something else, but what is different in Alberta is that they have claimed for over half a century that they are champions of free enterprise while their actions tell a different story.

Social Credit's successors, the Progressive Conservatives, were also remarkably flexible. Two days after Peter Lougheed was elected he stated: "We stand for free enterprise—not socialism. We stand for social reform and individual rights—not big government control" (quoted in Emery and Kneebone, 2005: 12). He did, however, believe that free enterprise needed at nudge. According to political scientist Allan Tupper, Lougheed was committed to private enterprise as an ideal but saw an active role for government:

> Textbook ideals about a narrow and restricted role for the provincial government made little sense in a province that was far away from major markets and population concentrations, that depended on natural resources, and that presided over valuable, but depleting, stocks of oil and natural gas (2004: 220).

Almost immediately after taking office, the government pointed out that the Social Credit government had made a serious error when it agreed to a 16.66% ceiling on royalties. After lengthy negotiations with the industry it came up with a new plan. However, to the chagrin of the industry, the government subsequently abolished the ceiling and announced that the royalty rate would rise with the price of oil. The decision was made in Cabinet with no consultation or warning (Richards and Pratt, 1979: 225).

Just as OPEC used oil as a political weapon, Alberta brandished it in federal-provincial battles over domestic prices. In that period the industry was sidelined. There was almost no consultation and Canadian Petroleum Association officials were informed that they were not needed and that their input was not required. "They were politely told to bow out" (Gill, 1985: 96).

The Conservatives bought Pacific Western Airlines in the hope that it could influence the scope and pace of development in the Arctic, making Edmonton the gateway to the north. It also entered into partnerships with the private sector via the Alberta Energy Company (which was 50% owned by the government), investing in tar sands projects and other energy-related ventures. Alberta Gas Trunk Line morphed into Nova which expanded its role and was used skilfully by the government as a tool to advance its province-building plans.

Like the Manning government which spent lavishly on roads, schools and services, the Lougheed government did the same. Supporters of small government might argue that money should not be overflowing from provincial coffers, that it should more properly be left in taxpayers' pockets. However, Albertans were proud of the superlative infrastructure, and at that time the discourse of tax cuts had not taken hold.

It seems that, like the Premier, the population was pragmatic: In the late 1970s, in a survey of Albertans, Gibbins found that they supported increased government spending across a wide range of programs. He commented that there was "little evidence to suggest that Albertans would like to rein in government spending and government expansion, in fact, the opposite appears to be the case" (1979: 158–59). Nevertheless, the belief persisted that Albertans were different and the perceived difference was invoked by provincial elites, the media and western separatists.

When Ralph Klein won the Conservative leadership campaign and embarked on a crusade to eliminate the deficit on the expenditure side of the ledger, he was praised for his courage. He appeared to have the right stuff to streamline government, lower taxes and intervene as little as possible in the economy. Less than a decade later, people were beginning to question his right-wing credentials. In a devastating critique, Andrew Nikiforuk (2002) dissected ten myths about the Premier in which he questioned Klein's faith in free markets and the claim that the Alberta government was no longer in the business of being in business.

Nikiforuk points out that while cutting spending on schools and hospitals in the early 1990s, Ralph Klein gave the oil and gas industry generous tax breaks or royalty holidays and subsidies to the tune of $314 million. In addition there was an annual $640 million subsidy in free water allocations to the industry and $4 billion in rebates to Albertans to cushion the effects of electricity deregulation. In the 2005 provincial budget "program spending is easily the highest in history" (*Insight*, 18: 30). These actions do not describe a government that has retreated from the marketplace.

Alberta and Saskatchewan are often regarded as having pursued very different ideological, and therefore economic, paths. As the two provinces were created by drawing a line on the map to produce roughly equal entities, they provide an interesting laboratory to study the effects of ideologically driven policy decisions. Economists Ronald Kneebone and Hugh Emery (2005) undertook a comparison of the sister provinces to establish whether the assumptions are correct. They point out that Saskatchewan is perceived as a socialist province whose CCF/NDP governments have favoured public ownership and participation in the economy. The consequence has been lower incomes and an underperforming economy. Alberta's right-wing governments, on the other hand, are seen as preferring the role of "passive rentiers"[4] content to collect resource rents while leaving the economy to private interests. In Alberta's case, higher incomes are seen as a result of letting the private sector get on with the job.

SOURCE: JOHN LARTER, ARTIZANS.COM

*Ralph Klein as the stereotypical Alberta cowboy.*

Kneebone and Emery's conclusion that might surprise some people:

> Our analysis shows that while the rhetoric of the leaders of the two provinces may have differed, in practice there has been little difference in the policies pursued by the governments of the two provinces with respect to the development of natural resources. Financial constraints and market forces limit the ability of socialist governments to be public entrepreneurs while times of abundance encourage even right-wing governments to move into the role of public entrepreneur (2005: 2).

---

4. A rentier is someone whose income is derived from shares, bonds, rents and other such assets.

They also concluded that "it is not obvious that Saskatchewan is an economic under-performer."

This brief summary of the behaviour of governments since the 1940s, which is when Social Credit is believed to have made a right turn, is to show the dissonance between words and deeds. The words were accepted uncritically and this contributed to the impression that Albertans like small government, abhor any "socialist" measures, and have a strong commitment to free enterprise. Provincial governments have generally been business friendly, although the Lougheed government sometimes disappointed Alberta's most important industry.

Political scientist Gurston Dacks makes an important point on the role that the province's main industries play. A major commodity, initially agriculture and then oil and gas, has provided the bread and butter for a large proportion of the population throughout the province's history. Consequently, it has become customary to identify the general interest of the population with the interests of that dominant commodity (1986: 188). In other words, the assumption has been that whatever is good for agriculture/the petroleum industry, is good for Alberta.

Provincial elites have fostered this viewpoint and have largely succeeded in elevating it to an article of political faith. Alberta's primary exports, agriculture and petroleum, have both attracted federal attention. Conflicts have arisen which have allowed the provincial government to champion the provincial interest with great vigour. Debate about intra-provincial issues was muted as Albertans regarded the most important battles as external, requiring them to give the provincial government the strongest mandate to fight its battle with its federal counterpart (Dacks, 1986: 187).

There were intense and acrimonious disputes with Ottawa during Aberhart's reign. Manning's style was very low-key but he protected the province's interests fiercely, especially with respect to natural gas. Lougheed's epic battles with Trudeau were played out in full colour on television, bringing them into people's living rooms. Klein's numerous disputes with the federal government are all a call to arms. Opposition parties are marginalized, there are few debates in the legislature, and the provincial government gallops to the defense of provincial interests. There is a uni-dimensional feel to this province because the internal differences are lost in the smoke of external battles.

Calgary and Southern Alberta have been strong supporters of the Conservatives for over three decades, but Edmonton's soil has been more fertile for opposition parties—earning it the name "Redmonton." Yet it seems that Calgary has branded the entire province with its (American) cowboy image and that is all that outsiders see.

As Claude Denis points out, there are many facets to the province's character, epitomized by Preston Manning (the preacher) and Ralph Klein (the cowboy or roughneck): "There are days when the preacher seems too grim and others when the cowboy judged [by the average person] too rowdy." However, both are part of the political landscape (1995: 91). It is important to stress once again that Albertans are not all of one mind. As is the case elsewhere, there are differing bodies of opinion and different world views. My contention is that a disproportionate amount of attention to the stereotypical Albertan has obscured other aspects of Alberta's political culture. The stereotype has been utilized by friend and foe alike, reinforcing the view that Albertans are a lumpen mass incapable of the critical thinking so essential in a democracy.

The main reason why Alberta projects this image is the sorry state of opposition parties (and I would venture to argue, of opposition itself) in the province. The combination of non-partisan sentiments, extreme loyalty to the "home team" even from the bulk of the media and very short legislative sessions has served to consign opposition parties to oblivion. More troubling is that, in the climate of consensus politics, there is a virtual silencing of dissent. In this respect, Albertans are unique. Although there are critics who challenge government actions, they are most often ignored by the media. The impression that the population is acquiescent is thus reinforced.

The thrust of my argument has been that the people of Alberta share fundamental values with citizens of other parts of the country. What this chapter has shown is that the similarities are overlaid by the discourse of difference promoted by provincial elites. Like people in other provinces, Albertans are concerned about the state of nursing homes, education and the environment. Despite numerous studies and recommendations on health care reform, the government is proceeding very cautiously. If it was confident of the self-reliance and individualism that are believed to characterize the population, a parallel private health care system would have been introduced years ago. Although (theoretically) in favour of greater public input via direct democracy, Albertans have not followed through on their beliefs.

The question one has to ask is whether it is true, as Mark Lisac (2004) has argued, that we are "soaked in self deception"? Are Calgarians in particular, with the highest rate of post-secondary education in the country, docile or just too comfortable? In the next few chapters I will attempt to explain how public opinion has been manipulated, and how narratives are fashioned and an Alberta identity constructed—an identity with mythical ingredients.

# 6

# Opinion Formation

Everywhere people meet and converse, ordinary citizens express their views on some fairly complex topics, such as stem cell research, global warming and genetic engineering. It would be a full-time job to research each of these specialized matters thoroughly even if someone had the inclination to do so. Yet it is rare to hear people admit that they lack the knowledge to comment on important issues of the day. How then do busy people form opinions; do they invest much time in information gathering? The question we will be exploring in this chapter is how citizens form their opinions on important matters.

In fact, it has been found that interest in and knowledge of major issues is sorely lacking in the population. In 1983, researchers concluded that "when confronted with policy debates of great and abiding interest to political elites many Americans can do no better than shrug" (Kuklinski and Hurley, 1983: 730). The situation in Canada is similar: research here has found that most political opinions are based on little political information, and often those views are internally contradictory (Dyck, 2000: 239). Researchers were concerned about the implications of these findings for representative democracy: How meaningful is democracy if ordinary people care little about the burning issues of the day? How does this affect democracy in Alberta?

## Cue-taking

The reputation of democratic polities has been partially salvaged by the work on cue-taking. Students of public opinion have found that individuals use shortcuts to compensate for their lack of knowledge (Zaller, 1992). Given that representative democracy requires a modicum of knowledge of important issues, the apparent indifference of a large majority of citizens has been a cause of concern and a topic of study for many scholars.

They have found that people take their cues from prominent individuals, or perhaps friends whom they respect and trust. Someone more knowledgeable and perhaps ideologically compatible who makes a statement provides a yardstick to assess the issue at hand and supplies the individual with a ready-made opinion. The reputation of the source of such a statement is so important that cue-taking citizens focus heavily on the "who," and the "what" recedes into the background—the messenger overwhelms the message (Kuklinski and Hurley, 1994: 773).

The authors point out that, although cue-taking is assumed to be a rational cognitive process by which decisions are made, emotions and visceral reactions play a major role. Interpreting statements in the abstract is very different from interpreting these messages if they are believed to emanate from a trusted individual (1994: 747).

Members of the farming community took their cues from Henry Wise Wood because he was well respected. His analysis of political parties and his party solutions were absorbed by the UFA membership, and even when group government and delegate democracy proved unworkable, his reputation remained intact.

During the Depression Albertans were desperate enough to support anything that was on offer. Aberhart stepped into the limelight at a time when Premier Brownlee was involved in a grubby paternity suit. Aberhart was a lay preacher, so his moral credentials were unassailable. Little wonder the people were willing to pin their faith in him and the seductive solution he had to solve their problems.

What is fascinating about the material on cue-taking is that researchers found that when they attributed statements to a particular individual, say John F. Kennedy, respondents supported it even if Kennedy would never have held those particular views. The importance of the source is illustrated by the running battle between Aberhart and Major Douglas.

Social Credit was a confusing, complex and convoluted economic and social analysis that Aberhart simplified, even vulgarized, according to his critics. With the help of charts and graphs, skits explaining "poverty in the midst of plenty" to a mystified Man from Mars and through his radio show, Aberhart generated a lot of interest in Douglas's arcane theory. In the process, he took considerable liberties with it but it did not matter to his followers.

Just before Douglas arrived to speak to a special committee of the provincial government in 1934, Aberhart resigned as leader of the movement. Douglasites had forced him out for what they considered were inaccurate interpretations of Social Credit. They arranged for the Great Man to speak at a public meeting in Calgary, and in a deliberate snub to Aberhart, Douglas spoke for two hours without a single reference to him. When the crowd realized Aberhart was not going to speak, there was a near riot and the meeting broke up in chaos. Apparently Douglas and Aberhart had a very heated argument in the cloakroom and called each other "very rude names" (Barr, 1974: 63). What this incident illustrates is that Aberhart's followers cared little for Douglas and his theory. They preferred Aberhart's simplified version and, more importantly, trusted him more than they did the boring and uninspiring Douglas. The messenger was certainly more important than the message.

There is a more contemporary example from the 1993 election campaign mentioned earlier, when Liberal leader Laurence Decore built his platform around the need to eliminate the deficit. He had identified this as a problem when the Tories were dismissing it. However, when Ralph Klein began to talk about deficit reduction voters heeded his message. Both the Liberals and the Conservatives prescribed more or less the same medicine, but Albertans reacted more favourably to Klein. They were willing to place their trust in the folksy Premier rather than Decore, who did not exude the same warmth as his opponent.

Our obsession with celebrity in the 21st century means that the endorsement of people like former sex-symbol Bridgette Bardot and Oprah Winfrey may be sufficient for some people to oppose the seal hunt or refrain from eating hamburgers. Elder and Cobb (1983: 6) point out that it may not be rational to rely on the status of the communicator to evaluate the merits of an idea. However, since people have limited information and little reason to search for more, it is not exactly irrational either. The importance of the source dovetails neatly with the media's preference for stories with a personal slant.

## The Media

There is a reciprocal relationship between the media focus on personalities and the dependence of citizens on the views of those individuals to form their opinions. Lance Bennett contends that because the news is personalized and focuses on attractive political personalities, it encourages the public to adopt a passive attitude, permitting those personalities to do their thinking and acting for them (1988: 23). However, before we judge the public too harshly, it should be pointed out that it is difficult and time-consuming to form opinions on important topics based on our own research. It would require becoming a "professional citizen"—i.e., giving up one's job to devote one's life to public interest research.

The media shapes the way we see the world, determining what subjects will be discussed and which are relevant for mass consumption. Referring to television news, Taras points out that it is a powerful conduit, presenting images as well as facts and values to viewers. It therefore plays a role in setting the political agenda and raising issues that become lodged in the public's consciousness (1990: 3). Unfortunately, it does not provide adequate analysis to assess events and issues. Bennett argues that the news presented by media is "superficial, narrow, stereotypical, propaganda-laden and of little explanatory value" (1988: 9).[1] It would thus be of limited use to listeners or viewers looking for in-depth analysis of current events. Some would question whether there is a market for in-depth analysis and critical debate, or whether the public gets the coverage it deserves.

The way in which messages are communicated also has an impact on the quality of public discourse. Although dealing with real events, coverage has all the hallmarks of fiction with dramatic images, emotional conflict and an emphasis on performance. The audience is treated to a

---

1. These rather strong statements are backed up with numerous examples (ranging from the Bay of Pigs and Watergate to US-Soviet relations) of the way in which events and issues were presented by the media.

steady diet of escapism, entertainment and superficial enlightenment, a situation that hardly generates vigourous debate (Black, 1982: 90). If the goal is entertainment, and in the contest for ratings it often seems to be, then the audience will become passive, uncritical and intellectually lazy. Is this also (or especially) the case in Alberta?

According to Roger Epp (1984) the Alberta media's attitude towards the government has evolved over the years from lukewarm towards the UFA, hostile towards early Social Credit, then respectful of Manning. Since the Progressive Conservatives took office, they have been very successful in managing and controlling the media and the message. Epp describes how Peter Lougheed used television to his advantage, enabling him to circumvent the media and talk directly to the people. (This is reminiscent of Aberhart's "Back to the Bible" radio broadcasts which gave him a direct channel of communication to his listeners.)

Television had become a very powerful medium when Peter Lougheed became Premier and he recognized its value. He conquered his initial discomfort with it and used it to good effect in televised addresses and at First Ministers Meetings. If Albertans were confused about where they stood they could certainly take their cues from a Premier who would take no guff from Ottawa. The Alberta media loved it and him. They gleefully recorded the encounters with Trudeau and Ontario Premier Bill Davis as Lougheed defended the province's natural resources.

Epp's contention is that Lougheed managed the media very well. He employed a number of tactics, from refusing to grant interviews to "eastern editors" to agreeing to go on open line shows only if questions were sent to him in advance and the program was taped. When faced with a difficult question he would ramble on in incomplete sentences, preventing journalists from getting a 30-second clip, or he would tap his pencil on the table to affect the sound quality (1979: 44).

The Public Affairs Bureau (PAB) was expanded during the Conservative administration and in 1982–83 it had a staff of 230. The Premier had a good relationship with CFCN TV in Calgary and a former reporter from CFRN in Edmonton (a CTV affiliate) claims he was instructed not to give NDP leader Grant Notley coverage on the station's popular six o'clock news. This was denied by the news and public affairs manager. However, another legislative reporter, Geoff Davy, states that it was an unwritten law that the NDP was relegated to the later newscast. He also commented that "[s]elf-censorship silences as effectively as government decrees" (quoted in Hustak, 191–92). During the energy and constitutional battles, journalists felt pressure to be loyal Albertans against Ottawa, when the need arose (Epp, 1984: 25).

Hustak contends that the media basically played on Lougheed's team in disputes with the federal government and were unwilling to disclose government failings because this would be viewed by the public as anti-Albertan (1979: 192). He explains why the Premier received almost unqualified support in the province:

> To understand Peter Lougheed is to understand Alberta, for more than any other Canadian Premier, including René Levesque, Lougheed is his constituency. There is an appealing squareness about the man, a genuine sincerity and aggressive confidence that enhances his credibility. He has come to personify the future—the elusive future that has inspired three generations of Albertans through colonialism, drought, depression and war. Lougheed's career and personality embody the emergence of Western Canada into the mainstream of Confederation (1979: 238).

When Ralph Klein became Premier, he proved to be very adept at controlling the message. This is not surprising as he is a former journalist and understands how the system works. He has expanded and reorganized the PAB so it is now centralized in the Premier's office and its budget in 2003–04 was $13 million. As PAB staff attend high-level department meetings, the Premier's office has the ability to monitor what is going on in every department (Sampert, 2005: 43). Hustak and Epp both comment on the degree of secrecy surrounding government during the Lougheed era and Sampert explains how, despite Freedom of Information and Privacy legislation, it is extraordinarily difficult to obtain information on the Klein government.

If the Alberta media has been largely uncritical of the government, at least since the Conservatives came into power, coverage of Alberta in the national media is often condescending and frequently invokes the clichéd Western motif of the cowboy. This gives credence to the dismissal of critical reporting as "Eastern Canadian propaganda." The press cheered on Peter Lougheed when he took on the federal government over energy and the constitution. As they supported the thrust of Ralph

Klein's deficit elimination campaign, they did not examine the underlying premises or the speed with which it was implemented. As filters of information, the media "constructs" the political reality we see or hear about, so the public has access only to what the press feels is newsworthy according to its criteria.

The work done on the role played by the media in "framing" issues reinforces the contention that citizens would find it difficult to arrive at informed decisions if they had to rely entirely on the mass media. Recurring themes on the media's role in shaping political debate relate to its propensity to emphasize style over substance, to oversimplify complex issues and to engage in sensationalism. In the past, it was only female politicians whose wardrobes received attention, but in the last few decades even males have come under such scrutiny and are praised or ridiculed based on their appearance.

Nowadays it is possible to read literally hundreds of newspapers and search for any number of topics on the internet. In the 1970s and early 1980s, this option was not available so the views of Albertans were shaped entirely by what the government told them, as reported faithfully by the press. I wonder how Albertans would have reacted if, after the NEP was unveiled, they were informed that Ontario had been forced to provide a market for unwanted Alberta oil, and had to pay more for it for over a decade. This was a result of the National Oil Policy, implemented in 1960, which divided the country at the Ottawa Valley line and reserved everything west of that for Alberta oil. This did not get a mention in media coverage.

It is difficult for people outside the province to appreciate the psychological boost provided by Alberta's oil wealth. The province had been in a quasi-colonial relationship with Ottawa for a quarter of century. In 1935 Aberhart had to go cap in hand to the national capital seeking a loan of $18 million which the province needed urgently. There was some doubt whether civil servants could be paid, as half of provincial revenue was ear-marked for debt repayment. Ottawa lent the province $2 million (Barr, 1974: 85). The province had become a laughingstock when a spate of Social Credit legislation was struck down by the courts, disallowed or reserved by the Lt. Governor. Even during prosperous times Alberta investors in the oil and gas industry had received a chilly reception when they sought to borrow money on Bay

Street. All of these memories were stored up, and when Alberta had something Ontario needed, Albertans were happy that the shoe was finally on the other foot.

Albertans were very glad to have a leader like Lougheed to present the face of modern Alberta. Journalists who were Albertans were therefore quite protective of his image. Albertans were also pleased when Klein's deficit reduction campaign was covered by prominent American newspapers like the *New York Times*.

## Focusing on Personalities

In addition to depending too heavily on prominent personalities for opinion, the focus on personalities, either public figures or private individuals who are victims or beneficiaries of a particular policy, has another consequence. It encourages the public to see events as isolated phenomena rather than to appreciate how they intersect and even converge with larger issues.

Take, for example, the group of farmers dissatisfied with the Canadian Wheat Board's monopoly on marketing wheat. Reports of their actions can be treated as a David and Goliath story, pitting a few puny farmers against a draconian Canadian institution. This is the easiest angle and provides the ingredients of an exciting melodrama.

In October 2002, when a group of farmers was jailed for taking grain over the border without a permit from the Board, there was a protest rally complete with speeches, musicians and a woman wearing prison stripes and a ball and chain. Also at the rally was Ralph Klein wearing an anti-Wheat Board cap—it provided a wonderful photo opportunity and some great sound bites. The Premier was there to denounce the Board for its monopoly and raise the possibility of a constitutional challenge.

Now this is an issue that polarizes people, but the superficial coverage it usually gets does not do the story justice. If it was approached in a different manner, farmers might think twice about the possibility of dismantling an institution that has served them well. The Board provides security for the farmer, and as a single-desk seller has negotiating power that individual farmers could never match. Its international reputation is so high because the Board is a reliable and consistent supplier.

Other questions the media might deal with are the trade-off between short-term benefits and long-term security: when farmers can sell in the US for a higher price than they get from the Board they will seize the opportunity. But what will happen when the price is low if they have a "choice"? Only in-depth treatment of this issue can convey its complexity and explain why a quick fix might create greater problems further along the road. Another pertinent question is why American farmers are so determined to eliminate the Board's monopoly.

However, the temptation is to tell a story that is charged with emotion, tears if possible, to rouse the public. "*People Magazine* journalism" (Taras, 1990) that highlights the human interest angle and mutes more abstract and important issues does not serve the audience well. The effect is the same as looking at a single shard of glass in a stained-glass window and trying to imagine the full picture.

## The Government's Role

Politicians and the media need each other and, if the media is guilty of superficiality and oversimplification, politicians are often their willing collaborators.[2] Although politicians are dependent on the media for favourable coverage, or any coverage, not all of them are helpless pawns. Politicians on government benches, especially First Ministers and Cabinet ministers, are newsworthy and it is possible for governments to exploit the media to attain their goals.

Alan Cairns (1974) reminds us that governments are not passive actors reacting to public demands as they are expressed. They shape their societies as much as the society shapes them. Some years later, Benjamin Ginsberg (1988: 6) made this point more forcefully, arguing that although there is a linkage between "the will of the people" and government action, we should remember that this "will" has also helped governments "domesticate" mass belief and harness it for their own purposes:

> While contemporary Western governments do listen and
> defer to their citizens' views, the public opinion to which

---

2. This is a vicious circle for politicians: Conscientious and competent politicians or candidates are not likely to attract media attention for these worthwhile qualities. Individuals are forced to surround themselves with attractive packaging, to be witty and/or controversial to ensure they will make news. This is a risk because the same reporters might mock at them as they struggle to improve their image by changing their hairstyles or getting rid of their glasses.

regimes bow so assiduously is not the natural and sponta-
neous popular force that confronted their predecessors.
Instead, the opinion that contemporary leaders heed is in
many respects an artificial phenomenon that national governments themselves helped to create and that their efforts
continue to sustain (1988: 32).

The media plays an important role in setting the agenda, but governments have the ability to mould public opinion and can to a certain
extent "manage" the media. The government of Alberta devotes a considerable amount of resources to this project through the Public Affairs
Bureau mentioned above.

## Opinion Creation

The idea that the opinions of ordinary citizens matter is a democratic
one. In the past monarchs and despots cared little about their subjects.
Citizens in democracies today are consulted often, their views are canvassed on a number of issues. This suggests that public opinion is an
important determinant of political decisions, but is this really the case?
In a discussion about the manipulation of opinion, political scientist
Walter Truett Anderson, like Ginsberg, refers to the creation of the
"general will" and argues that:

> [t]he great games of modern politics, the by-products of
> democracy that often threaten to destroy everything democ-
> racy was meant to be, are the games of opinion moulding:
> propaganda, brainwashing, programming and deprogram-
> ming, advertising and public relations. Games of reality
> making (1990: 116).

Before discussing how governments "create" opinion, it will be
instructive to explore opinion creation in other spheres. No other field
provides more raw material for this topic than the advertising and public relations sector from which many government "spin doctors" are
recruited. The *raison d'être* of this industry is persuasion, and with the
technological wizardry available, the task of its practitioners is much
easier. Persuading people to choose one particular brand of detergent
requires a campaign emphasizing its merits over that of its rivals.
Whether the product is, in fact, superior may be hard to prove and, in
any case, does not have earth-shattering consequences. However, when

an entire industry, such as the logging or nuclear industry, embarks on a major public relations offensive to alter public perceptions, the matter shifts to a different dimension.

The power to shape public opinion is demonstrated by the strategies adopted by the nuclear industry in the United States and Britain, specifically by the nuclear power plants, Florida Light & Power (FP&L) and Scottish Nuclear Limited (SNL). Tilson (1996) documents the efforts of these plants to create a favourable public climate for nuclear power by promoting it as an environmentally friendly alternative to fossil fuels.

The author observes that the ebb and flow of issues can be viewed "to be largely the work of promoters who package and present them and, in fact, define them as problems" (1996: 65). Anxious to replace memories of Chernobyl and Three Mile Island with a more positive image, both companies have embarked upon "makeovers" that capitalize on the "greening" of public sentiment.

Tilson traces the transformation in tactics from reactive to proactive, from damage control to explicit attempts to promote nuclear energy as benign and beneficial to the environment. Both companies have opened visitor centres to demonstrate that the industry has nothing to hide and, in fact, cares deeply about the environment.[3] The Florida centre is high-tech, hands-on and interactive, consistent with the expectations of children and adults today. With a lovable animated pirate-parrot ("Hutch"), visitors explore the nuclear paradise. This slick campaign is very seductive:

> That Hutch and his high-tech wonderland should be so reminiscent of Disney World in Orlando (where one of the most popular attractions, "Pirates of the Caribbean," features animated pirates and talking parrots) further accentuates the fun-filled atmosphere of the centre. Through its promotional imaging, FP&L seeks to simulate Disney World, which has come to epitomize [according to an analyst of the Disney's goal] "family fun, childhood enchantment, and the story of

---

3. FP&L has received awards, including one from the Audubon Society, for is environmental leadership. What visitors to these centres do not know is that most of the research and monitoring for example of sea turtles and crocodiles, is required by federal and state agencies.

America as Freedom and Progress, itself written as the story
of the world" (Tilson, 1996: 73).

The SNL centre strives to be equally attractive to visitors with
exhibits, interactive displays and a coastal walk punctuated with panels
providing details on the coast, wildlife and the nuclear station. Both
companies feel that their centres have succeeded in changing public
perceptions and this is not surprising, as their visitors are responding to
selective facts about nuclear power.

As we will see, governments too can carefully select the information
that they present to citizens. When governments engage in public persuasion campaigns, the resources at their disposal are formidable and the
consequences potentially far-reaching. Noting the growing use of advertising to persuade citizens, Jonathan Rose (writing about federal advertising) observes that in taking complex ideas and reducing them to simple images, advertising commodifies politics, and this debases "our political discourse and relegate[s] politics to the grammar of advertising"
(Rose, 1994).

So how do governments go about constructing public opinion? As we
have seen, they do not merely respond to public opinion. There are at
least two ways in which governments can shape public opinion, first by
identifying priorities (agenda setting), and second by defining them in
ways that citizens will support.

Identifying priorities may appear to be a perfectly straightforward
exercise requiring no more than making a list of what needs to be done.
Despite Premier Klein's use of such an analogy, running a province is not
as simple as running a household and it takes more effort than making
a grocery list or drawing up a family budget. Multiple and often conflicting demands emerge from groups within a society, and ultimately it is
Cabinet that chooses which will receive attention. Some things make it
onto the political agenda and others do not. In addition to being manageable, the priorities must also be arranged in a hierarchy—the
sequence is subject to rearrangement.

When Premier René Levesque lost the sovereignty referendum in
Quebec in 1980, his government believed that economic uncertainty
contributed to the number of people who voted "No." The government's top priority became building up the Quebec economy so
Quebecers would have greater confidence in their ability to go it alone.

Sovereignty-association yielded its place on the top of the agenda to one further down the list. Former Premier Lucien Bouchard adopted a similar strategy.

Political leaders determine what they want to address. When Manning became Premier, he defined his priorities as reconstruction of the economy and eradicating the stigma of Alberta having defaulted on its debts. To that end he was determined to pay bondholders in full for the bonds on which the province defaulted in 1936. There were many critics who argued that this was unnecessary, but he won them over. Quite apart from restoring the financial integrity of the province, there was also concern that when the province needed to borrow again, its credit rating would be poor. He dealt with this matter successfully and skilfully (Watkins, 1980: 152–53).

Klein's main priority was elimination of the deficit, and then the debt, and it took a sustained effort on the government's part to ensure Albertans absorbed the message. Constant repetition that there was a spending problem, not a revenue problem, had the desired effect. Soon polls showed that the people believed the deficit to be the most serious issue in provincial politics and that they had to tighten their belts. Some critics have pointed out that the deficit and debt were manageable and were certainly not a crisis; this brings to mind a comment by political scientist Murray Edelman, who also writes about constructing public opinion. He contends that leaders play on the emotions of the public by framing issues so people are "aroused by images of problems and reassured by promised solutions" (quoted in Bennett, 1988: 108).

In the campaign to eliminate the deficit, the Klein government evoked images of future generations bowed down by debt. The issue of indebtedness speaks to Albertans whose parents and grandparents struggled with mortgages during the Depression or, worse, lost their farms. The shameful memory of the province defaulting on its debt can also be added to the mixture of emotions. All these memories helped persuade the population that action was vital. Governments mine the past in their quest for symbols that will resonate with the population.

## Definitions
Having set priorities, governments then have to convince people that the issues they have singled out require urgent attention and this is

where definitions come into play. It is possible for situations to be defined in a way that will evoke public anxiety, and "policy-makers play a central role in this definition process, interpreting events to suit their own purposes..." (Elder and Cobb, 1983: 24). Manipulation of the public is most blatant when a country is at war, but it should come as no surprise that, on a routine basis, governments are engaged in selling public policies using many of the techniques employed by marketing agencies. In the process, definitions come to play a major role. With language, definitions are used to construct political reality, and the most crucial definition is that of reality itself.

How often have you heard a remark from a public official that goes something like this: "we would really like to do such-and-such but the reality is..." Although it may sound strange, the "reality to which we respond is socially constructed" (Elder and Cobb, 1983: 143) and the ingredients are language and the symbols that are employed by policy makers. It is the perception of some phenomenon—how we define it—that spurs us to action or encourages us to ignore it.

Feminists are aware of the importance of definitions in shaping attitudes and one they question is the definition of the private sphere. If something is deemed to belong to the private sphere, then it does not concern society as a whole. If what goes on within a family, for example, is considered a private matter, then the government will not intervene.[4] Feminists have fought to prove that what takes place in the bosom of the family e.g. spousal violence, can and does have implications for society as a whole and that the community pays the price of dysfunctional family relationships. The point to keep in mind is that re-defining a particular phenomenon alters our view as to whether it is acceptable or not and, in the instance just cited, whether it is appropriate and necessary to intervene or not.

A personal experience illustrates very nicely how definitions can be deployed to influence behaviour. Frustrated with squirrels that were girdling and killing the branches of a tree in our back yard, I sought advice from a field naturalist. She suggested a few remedies which we

---

4. There are aspects of private relationships that are regulated, such as marriage and divorce. There has also been a shift in thinking about the public/private divide in recent decades, partly because of the efforts of the women's movement.

had already tried and then pointed out that they are descendants of two Ontario squirrels that escaped from the Calgary Zoo and multiplied. The other two nuggets of information she shared were that they had displaced native squirrels and were not a protected animal. Therefore, they could be trapped and... The next step was left dangling. By this point she was completely out of patience with me and she snapped: "They're just rodents with bushy tails, you know."

Now, the word "rodent" conjures up all kinds of unpleasant images—creatures which spread the plague and are generally nasty. This would be an effective turn-off for most people, and they would not feel so squeamish about dispatching these creatures. I mention this incident because it demonstrates so perfectly how a speaker can alter the perception of the listener by evoking images that are either disgusting or inspiring in an attempt to influence behaviour. The goal is to redefine someone or something to produce the desired behaviour. Definitions are crucial and they are also fluid.

Ignatieff argues that in the former Yugoslavia ethnic differences *per se* were not responsible for the nationalist politics that emerged. "Consciousness of ethnic nationalist hatred only surfaced when surviving communist elites, beginning with Serbia, began manipulating nationalist emotions in order to cling to power" (1993: 16–17). Ethnicity defined how people should be treated, and because ethnic solidarity became the only factor that could be used to mobilize people, it was recruited to drive a wedge between groups.

Every society has cleavages that separate one group from another. Whether these flow from differences in income, religion, race and/or language, the fault lines may lie dormant until the differences become politicized, i.e., they become the basis of claims on the system. In Canada, region is one such fault line which is exploited periodically by political elites making symbolic appeals to the population when the need arises.

## Symbols

A provincial population, like any other group that lives together for any length of time, will share innumerable experiences. The collective memory is studded with recollections of past glories or humiliations which bind people together. As these events become more remote and memories more hazy, they can assume important symbolic significance. The symbol comes to stand for something, tugging at underlying emotions. People are conditioned to respond to these culturally ingrained symbols which communicate messages without spelling out the allusion. They provide a cue and the response is predictable. One potent symbol in Alberta is the NEP, which rekindles outrage every time it is mentioned.

Symbols are crucial because they shape the way we see and understand political life. Symbolic and linguistic devices are employed "to soothe the public, blunt conflict and divert attention from material inequalities" (Edelman, 1964: 243). Thayer argues that resorting to symbolism is the most powerful of three propaganda tactics (the others are simplicity and repetition), as it is a type of emotional shorthand which enables the recipient to pick up allusions instantly: "The most enduring symbols are those that relate to the mythological underpinnings of groups" (1998: 10).

In politics, symbols can be manipulated to appeal to the electorate and, if they are used skilfully, they can be very useful in ensuring citizens view issues in a certain way. Conversely, failing to press the right buttons can pose a problem. One example of this is cited by Elder and Cobb (1983: 4–6) in their discussion of the differing reactions to very similar proposals presented by Richard Nixon and Senator George McGovern in 1969. Both dealt with welfare reform and entailed expansion of benefits but Nixon emphasized the work incentive features, calling it "workfare," not "welfare." He emphasized that it would enable families to be lifted out of poverty into self-sufficiency. The idea was favourably received by the public, but Nixon quietly dropped it because of Congressional opposition. However, McGovern's proposed guaranteed annual income, which was very similar, was greeted with ridicule. The authors argue that McGovern did not frame the proposal in language emphasizing positive American symbols and traditional values like self-sufficiency. This example illustrates that words and phrases have connotations which determine how they will be received. They can be deployed to promote unity or sow discord.

During the Klein government's deficit reduction campaign when the goal was to slash spending, the message was hammered home that borrowing to pay the bills was reckless and irresponsible, and spending had to be severely curtailed. Fiscal prudence was the watchword and "Klein the Knife" became a symbol, blazing a trail for others to follow. At the time, no distinction was made between the government equivalent of borrowing for a mortgage (or to pay for post-secondary education) and taking out a loan to go to Hawaii. When the revenue picture changed, the government began to restore some of the funding that had been cut, but this was defined as "reinvestment" because "spending" had negative connotations. The possibility of borrowing to pay for infrastructure was raised by the Infrastructure Minister in August 2005, and it was immediately denounced.

These examples illustrate the difficulty a government might have when it invests political resources to persuade the population about the need for some course of action and then has to change course. The Klein government is hoist by its own petard: having cultivated the image of fiscal prudence and garnered a lot of praise for it, in the new financial climate what can it do to justify spending again?

## Influencing Albertans

It is not difficult to see how the different factors we have been discussing play out within the context of Alberta politics, so it is not necessary to connect all the dots.

Albertans have had many outstanding Premiers who have been fierce champions of provincial rights. In these skirmishes, political leaders were defining reality for the population and providing them with cues. Securing these rights has been a major goal for successive governments.

Albertans have rewarded their political leaders with remarkable loyalty for almost nine decades. In part, this has been because they have been conditioned to focus their attention on the national arena in order to be ready to do battle. They have taken cues from provincial leaders and accepted their version of reality. However, this quiescence is also a result of affluence for most of the last half a century. When people are comfortable with the status quo, they are not likely to rebel as they did in 1921 and during the Depression. When Alberta's economy went bust in the 1980s, the Alberta government was able to blame it on the NEP. Although the NEP played a role in the downturn, it is also true that the main culprit was the collapse of the world price of oil which caused drilling rigs in Texas and Oklahoma to stand idle.

The discussion in this chapter shows the various ingredients that contribute to the formation of public opinion in the province. Opinions are not as stable as values, but it is apparent that Alberta governments have, over the years, revived painful memories to mobilize the population. What this has produced is a population that is permanently on orange alert for any incoming threat to the province's interests. This has been accomplished by telling a unique Alberta Story, a story that differs from the Canadian Story. The latter will be my next concern.

# 7

# Constructing a Canadian Identity

R eams have been written about the Canadian identity and the difficulty in defining it. One problem is where one should one start:
should we begin when Europeans first arrived or before the First Nations
societies were disturbed by European settlers? As we shall see, the term
"First Nations" has only recently come into use, and this is one indica-
tion of the fluidity of definitions and perceptions. In one sense an identity is a given: i.e. race, sex and caste are individual characteristics that
one is born with or into. The bases of a group identity may be ethnicity,
language and culture, but identities can be multiple and this is where
the idea of "construction" comes in. When people are asked to define
themselves they will often choose a characteristic that is most important
to them, perhaps gender, language or religion—there are many layers
from which to choose. Like individuals, nations have a layered identity
and they can be selective about the components that are used as the raw
materials in constructing one. Sometimes the identity owes much to
myth and historical interpretation. This is particularly true of "new"
nations. It will be instructive to take a look at the process of identity
construction and reconstruction in other places before turning our
attention to Canada and then Alberta.

As mentioned in the chapter on political culture, the values and attitudes that are shared in a society provide the glue that bind people together. Bonds like race and language define some nations, but there are not many countries that are homogeneous. The sociological reality of a nation may be that cultural, linguistic and other divisions exist, and it is necessary to find common ground that cuts across these cleavages. In the process of seeking that common ground, the people need to tell a story about themselves, a foundational narrative that defines the community they once were or that they want to become. There are several examples from the recent past.

As a result of the post-communist transition in Eastern Europe, many new political entities have emerged and, as they struggle to define themselves, there has been a tremendous resurgence of interest in "invented" and "imagined" communities. Historians, sociologists, political scientists and others have a wealth of material to work with as these new nations are inventing or re-inventing themselves.

There is some fascinating material emerging from these living laboratories which are providing insights into the processes that accompany the birth of a new nation. These countries do not have the luxury of time for the glue to evolve slowly, so the process of constructing a collective identity is accelerated. Levesque describes the impact this acceleration of history has: "The equilibrium between the present and the past is severely disrupted as traditions and heritage practices long taken for granted are falling apart" (2005: 349). Drawing on the past can be quite tricky in some situations when there are (literally) historical skeletons aplenty in the closet.

The Yugoslavian example is a fascinating one. One of the successor states of the former Austrian monarchy, it contained Serbs, Croats and Slovenes. After World War II the new socialist state included ethnic groups that had fought on both sides, so it was a challenge to ensure they coexisted. Ethnic tensions were suppressed during the reign of President Tito but after his death in 1980 they flared up. As mentioned in the previous chapter, Ignatieff (1993) contends that ethnicity was recruited to mobilize groups. The tragedy that has played out in the last few decades has resulted in the disintegration of the former Yugoslavia into a number of other "successor" states including Serbia.

Jovan Byford (2004) relates how Serbia is rewriting its history and, in the process, rehabilitating contentious historical figures. One of these is the late Bishop Velimirovic, who was considered a brilliant scholar in the 1920s. His goal at that point seemed to be to modernize the Church, but that all changed a few years later. His subsequent actions earned him a reputation for anti-Semitism and anti-Westernism. He rejected modern ideas like democracy and religious tolerance and considered Nazi Germany a positive role model. Yet he has become an icon for Serbs. Until the mid-1980s the Bishop was considered a traitor and a villain in Yugoslavia, but since then his status has altered and the Serbian Orthodox Church has canonized him. His rehabilitation was accomplished by an extreme makeover of his biography, which ignores his inflammatory writings and extreme views.[1] I mention this case as it exemplifies the powerful drive to create a flattering self-portrait that can speak to an extremely beleaguered group in need of heroes for the new national mythology. As historian Peter Seixas puts it: "A society whose traditions are fractured and challenged spends more energy on reconstructing a heritage to believe in" (2000).

A number of scholars who have written about nationalism, which flows from national identity, have stressed elements like invention (Hobsbawm, 1983) and imagination (Anderson 1983). However, creation myths and foundational narratives may not be universally accepted and are sometimes challenged by counter-narratives. The latter refer to the possibility of resistance to the narrative, but if those who oppose it are not very powerful, the dominant narrative will prevail. An example of such a situation comes from Belarus which became independent in 1990 with the collapse of the Soviet Union.

Two opposing narratives have been utilized to appeal to the population: supporters of now-President Lukashenka, used a familiar vocabulary which was not overtly Communist. It had huge resonance because the security it promised was comforting in the uncertain times faced by the population. Words and phrases used by the forces of democracy did not strike a chord with the population and Hungarian scholar Anna Brzozowska explains why. She points out that the difficulty faced by the pro-democracy supporters flows from the fact that their audience cannot

---

1. In addition to subscribing to the Jewish conspiracy theory, he believed that the Serbs were guards at the gates of "Aryan Europe."

relate to a group that extols the virtues of democracy using language they do not recognize. Their utterances are unfamiliar "[hence] the main misunderstanding: what the sender of the message sees as the promise of a better life, of more dignity and justice, the recipient sees as something strange to his or her experience, something representing danger and instilling fear" (2003: 50). The recitation of abstract principles, no matter how noble-sounding, leaves them unmoved. Another key point made by Brzozowska is that the pro-Lukashenka camp had control of public institutions, including education and the mass media, resources that their opponents lacked. Not surprisingly, the latter's competing narrative failed.

So how does this apply in the Canadian case? Do we have a foundational narrative and is it widely accepted? And is there a consensus about it in the country? How has the Canadian narrative changed over time?

## The Story of Canada
People have often lamented the lack of poetry and vision in the establishment of Canada. "Establishment" is the operative word because the original partners to Confederation formed a union out of necessity. In a sense it was a shotgun wedding forced on them by Britain which did not want to defend its North American colonies any longer. There were also economic and political reasons which played a role. The basis of the relationship was pragmatic and there were no starry-eyed visions of what they hoped to achieve together. Thus, when the Fathers of Confederation drafted the British North America Act, it lacked stirring and inspiring phrases and read more like a prenuptial agreement.

To tell a good story you need the right ingredients to stir the imagination. A revolutionary war does provide a tangible milestone and crystallizes memories but, unlike the Americans, we did not have one. Also, we have no Declaration of Independence, no sod house-to-Sussex Drive myth; no one has seen fit to analyse Speeches from the Throne, and if someone did, s/he would find the cupboard bare. Although political speeches today do contain a fair number of "lofty statements," they usually fall on stony ground. This could be because the people have little patience with rhetoric drafted by professional speech-writers or that it is too late to coin phrases with the right amount of emotional content to enshrine them as symbols.

Trudeau's slogan, "the Just Society," springs to mind immediately as an example of a phrase that had the potential to become part of the political vocabulary. It did not because Canadians took it as a pledge and were disappointed when it did not materialise. This state of affairs illustrates very nicely a point that Murray Edelman (1964) made about the importance of the remoteness of symbols. He argues that for a symbol to be potent it must be remote, set apart, impossible to check against reality. Edelman labels such devices "condensation symbols" and points out that they evoke emotions associated with a situation and "condense into one symbolic event, sign or act patriotic pride, anxieties, remembrances of past glories or humiliations, promises of future greatness" (1964: 5–6).

If the words "just society" had been used by one of the Fathers of Confederation (a rather anonymous lot), or had been part of the preamble in the Constitution Act of 1867, they would today be just as compelling as Jefferson's famous phrase about the right to "life, liberty and the pursuit of happiness."[2] Since we have few golden words from the past and politicians today must spell out to reporters and the public precisely what they mean, it will be difficult to invent a set of symbols at this stage.

National heroes, the flag and the anthem are other potential sources of symbols, but in Canada they have often divided rather than unified the population. (Although the flag has become a very proud symbol for Canadians, especially when they travel, it was contentious when it was first introduced.) Another major symbol, the monarchy, has less resonance with Canadians and never did resonate in Quebec. With regard to history, the most striking fact is that French-speaking and English-speaking Canadians remember historical events in quite different ways. The Commission on Bilingualism and Biculturalism found that French-speaking Canadians considered Durham[3] the great assimilator, Riel a

---

2. If Thomas Jefferson were uttering those words today, he would, shortly thereafter, have to explain into a forest of microphones and cameras, what exactly he meant, how he defined each term and how the government was going to implement its policy!

3. Lord Durham was sent to Canada in 1838 to investigate the causes of the conflict that had erupted in Upper and Lower Canada. He was appointed Governor General but resigned after five months. He famously said that in Lower Canada, he found "two nations warring in the bosom of a single state" and recommended the union of the two Canadas. The goal was to assimilate the French Canadians, as they were outnumbered by English-speaking Canadians.

defender of human rights who was murdered by the English, and conscription an unnecessary step that dragged the French into a conflict of concern only to those of British origin. To English-speaking Canadians on the other hand, Durham is a great de-colonizer, Riel a traitor and conscription a necessity (cited in Manzer, 1974: 147).

Anthropologist Ernest Gellner (1983: 36) emphasizes the importance of education in the creation of national identities. It is via the transmission of culture through education that children become aware of culturally significant elements which they internalize. This is the process of political socialization through which individuals acquire values, opinions, and information about the political system. It is an ongoing process which starts in the family and then expands to schools, peers, the media and so on. One of the most important agents of political socialization is the school system, but as the provinces have jurisdiction over education, each will emphasize different aspects of Canadian history in social studies curricula. Political scientist Rand Dyck points out the problem is compounded because "the forces of dualism [French and English], regionalism and continentalism in Canadian society make it difficult for the school system to develop any pan-Canadian sense of national identity" (2002: 127).

In a country as large and as diverse as Canada, it would be unwise not to mention undesirable, to suggest that we adopt a uniform, national curriculum that imposes a sort of canon to be taught across the country. An experience in Western Canada illustrates how fraught with problems this is.

In 1993 the four western provinces and three territorial governments embarked upon an unprecedented project to design common curriculum frameworks, the Western Canada Protocol, in core subjects including social studies (Richardson, 2004). Although there were practical problems to overcome, like differences in province-wide testing and texts, in Math and English Language Arts they were able to work out an acceptable compromise—but Social Studies presented a stumbling block. Here again, some of the difficulties were practical, but ultimately, in the fall of 2001, the program was completely abandoned. Questions of national identity presented the greatest difficulties and Richardson concludes that "the failure of the Protocol to establish any kind of consensus view of national identity suggests the complexities of implementing social studies curricula—even those limited to regionally based identities—that do not reflect local or provincial realities" (2002).

Given the numerous gaps in the Canadian story, it is remarkable that the country has not yet disintegrated, but there are intangible bonds that hold Canada together.

If history is problematic, geography is more promising: the Canadian landscape has lodged itself in the nation's collective psyche, but not without some help. Geographer Brian Osborne argues that a powerful symbolic attachment to the landscape (especially the north and the wilderness) has been developed so successfully that it has been transformed into a "patriotic topography" (2001: 12). Canadians take pride in the pristine landscape which has also become a metaphor for freedom and room to breathe on an increasingly crowded planet. Cynics point out that the environment is far from pristine and that the vast majority of people huddle together in cities. Nevertheless, the wilderness is never far away and the sometimes terrifying beauty of the landscape inspires and humbles Canadians today as it did previous generations. Unlike other symbols, the pull of the land is unambiguous and unifying, crossing linguistic, cultural and regional boundaries.

Geography also divides Canadians by inserting natural barriers like vast spaces between settlements, mountains and lakes. Enormous advances in technology that facilitate travel and communication have enabled us to deal with physical distances, but the psychological barriers remain.

The trouble with Canada is that it is an untidy place on which it is difficult to impose order—in fact that is part of its charm. It has not been possible to utilize the US model—i.e., to design the mould into which immigrants are poured and out of which they emerge as "Americans." The melting pot was a non-starter in Canada, as French-Canadians would have resisted it immediately. Other candidates were discarded along the way: at one time the narrative described Canada as a northern country of northern European people. (Canada's original inhabitants were conveniently omitted.) The "two founding peoples" (the French and the English) myth was (still is, in the minds of some Canadians) part of the Canadian narrative. This got mixed up with the "compact theory" of Canadian federalism with parties on either side of the linguistic divide defining it in a different way. For Quebec, it was a compact between the French and the English, but for the other provinces it was a compact between the provinces and the federal government that created the federation. Belatedly there has been recognition that if we are to talk about founding peoples, the First Nations should certainly be included and this is slowly creeping into the Canadian narrative.

The Great Canadian Story which could have been told to promote social cohesion and instill patriotic pride eludes us. The complexity of Canada's origins makes the task of constructing such a tale enormously difficult. A major difficulty with the storyline is, of course, the chasm between Quebec and the other provinces.

A number of issues divided French and English in Canada in the first half-century after Confederation: e.g. Louis Riel, the issue of French schooling in Manitoba[4] and conscription. After that Quebec and its population did not register on Canada's radar screen. Thus, until the Quiet Revolution in Quebec in 1960, the rest of Canada was oblivious to the dissatisfaction that was brewing in that province. The Quiet Revolution represented a transformation of Quebec from a religious, inward-looking society to a secular, outward-looking province determined to catch up and even surpass the rest of Canada. It gave voice to the disillusionment of Francophones with their place in Canada and, as a consequence, the provincial government began to make demands on Ottawa. The population in the rest of Canada suddenly realized that all was not well in *la belle province* which had isolated itself for decades.

After 1960, Quebec soared to the top of the political agenda and the question on everyone's lips was "What does Quebec Want?.." Four and a half decades later, while that is no longer the central question in Canadian politics, the Quebecois are still dissatisfied with their place in Confederation. The existence of Quebec with its overwhelmingly French-speaking population has prevented the notion of a pan-Canadian identity from taking root. To complicate matters, before the Quebec question could be understood, much less addressed, the western provinces, led by Alberta, began to become more assertive. As the

---

4. Historians consider the Manitoba Schools Question a watershed in Canadian federalism, one which choked off French migration to the west. This involved a dispute about Catholic (French) schooling in the province, which was dismantled in 1890 despite constitutional guarantees.

"French fact" did not reflect reality of daily life in the West, there was some resentment in the region towards the policy of Bilingualism that the Trudeau government adopted in 1970.[5]

During constitutional negotiations in the 1970s and 1980s, the principle of ten equal provinces began to be articulated more forcefully, a natural extension of the compact theory espoused outside Quebec. This manifested itself in discussions on an amending formula in the 1970s. Before the

SOURCE: GLENBOW ARCHIVES M-8000-64

*Premier Peter Lougheed views Prime Minister Pierre Trudeau's proposed constitutional reforms as a waste of time. Tom Innes's cartoon appeared in the* Calgary Herald, *March 4, 1977.*

Constitution Act of 1982, amendments had to be made in Britain on a request from Ottawa. When previous negotiations on an amending formula had taken place, it was assumed that, because of their size, Quebec and Ontario should have a veto over constitutional amendments. However, the smaller provinces no longer felt that this was appropriate and, as a result, the amending formula which was proposed by Alberta was entrenched in the constitution.[6]

This formula does not provide the two Central Canadian provinces

---

5. Curiously, soon after that, when French immersion schooling became available across the country, parents in Calgary would camp outside schools overnight to ensure their children got one of the limited number of spaces available.

6. The formula for most amendments is the so-called 7/50 formula, which means that an amendment needs the support of 7 out of 10 provinces which have over 50% of the population.

with the power to reverse constitutional amendments. Since 1982, the constitution has received its Canadian citizenship so to speak, and there is no longer a need to go cap in hand to the British to ask their legislature to make changes.[7] The amending formula can be seen as a (re)assertion of the ten equal provinces view of Confederation that has pitted it against the Two- or Three- Founding Nations version of the Canadian narrative. What the emerging discourse does is to downgrade the status of Ontario, as its only claim to special treatment is that it contains 37% of the population. Given the electoral clout this confers, it is perhaps sufficient reward requiring no other recognition.

The Charter of Rights and Freedoms that is now embedded in the Constitution Act of 1982 is a source of great pride for Canadians, but it has also had another effect. Because it protects the rights of groups like women as well as linguistic and ethnic minorities, it has created a constituency that does not have a territorial base. In other words, there is every incentive for women, for example, to see themselves as right-bearers regardless which province they live in. The same goes for groups that might face discrimination in their search for jobs or housing. Some of these groups have national organizations and look to the national government to protect their interests. The salience of region for these "Charter" groups has diminished. Arguably, this is also true of environmental groups who have a pan-Canadian if not a planetary vision for protection of the environment.

To this point I have been arguing that it is difficult to construct a unifying narrative for Canada because of linguistic, regional and cultural differences that exist. However, a new narrative is being written and has slowly taken hold. It is a narrative that makes a virtue of our differences instead of lamenting them. What Canada exemplifies is what Richard Gwyn (1994) describes as a "post-modern" nation that is inclusive, diverse and tolerant. In other words, it is a country that has come to terms with the "age of migration" as Prime Minister Paul Martin described it in a speech in 2004.

A cornerstone of our claim to being a post-modern society is tolerance

---

7. There is some unfinished business on the constitutional front, as Quebec was the only province that was not a signatory to it. Two attempts to bring the province into the constitutional fold have not succeeded.

of difference. A major indicator of that tolerance is multiculturalism, a policy adopted by the Trudeau government in 1971. The impetus came from the Royal Commission on Bilingualism and Biculturalism which published its voluminous report in 1969. The Commission was reminded by immigrants who were neither English nor French in origin that they, too, were part of the Canadian family. Section 27 of the Charter entrenched the preservation and enhancement of Canada's multicultural heritage, and the Multicultural Act passed by the Mulroney government in 1988 strengthened the commitment to Canada's cultural diversity.

Thanks to the "we're all immigrants" element in the national narrative, Canada has been more welcoming of immigrants, including those from visible minority groups, than other Western countries. Some critics contend that the policy was just a device to put French-speaking Canadians in their place, but, if the motives were cynical, the policy has taken on a life of its own and is now spoken of approvingly. Despite some resistance to multiculturalism which lingers to this day, young people in Canada consider it enriching and heartily approve.

What Canada is moving towards is the triumph of civic over ethnic nationalism. The title of Michael Ignatieff's 1993 book, *Blood and Belonging*, sums up the basis of ethnic nationalism. The ties are based on ancestral characteristics such as race, language and culture and they are ancient. Civic nationalism, on the other hand, implies a more nebulous bond which flows from a set of values, a set of aspirations and a voluntary coming together of diverse people. As mentioned above, Canada is emphatically a country of immigrants, many of whom would not have set foot here if the First Nations had a strict immigration policy! So is the United States, and it too has woven this characteristic into its national narrative. However, instead of the Canadian mosaic, the US has opted for the melting pot and the Horatio Alger myth (that by dint of hard work anyone can succeed in the US).

Although some might argue that ethnic nationalism is alive and well in Quebec, even in that province multiculturalism has penetrated society. This accounts for the phenomenon of "ethnic separatists"—i.e., individuals from minority ethnic groups who support an independent Quebec. Canada's new Governor General, who was born in Haiti, was accused of having separatist sympathies.

In my opinion, the success of multiculturalism—and I do not want to exaggerate the extent to which it is embraced—has a great deal to do with the adoption of the Canadian Charter of Rights and Freedoms a scant decade after the multicultural policy was implemented in Canada. Ironically, if the Constitution Act of 1867 had contained a Charter, it might have remained a symbol rather than an instrument for citizens to secure their rights. This was not a remote symbol, so it could be checked against reality; hence its success. As it is, the rights conferred by the Charter were taken seriously and pursued skilfully by various groups. It has assumed significance not only as an instrument to secure rights, but as a document that symbolizes the values Canadians share.

Multiculturalism is now part of public discourse and, as Resnick explains, it "entails a re-definition of the national 'we' in a more universalistic way, rejecting ethnic origin, race, colour or religion as criteria for inclusion." He also points out that in a cross-national survey of sources of national pride done for UNESCO, Canadians were most supportive of cultural diversity (2005: 58–59).

Whether by accident or design, the Canadian story is emerging and it tells of a people that are drawn from over one hundred countries living in relative harmony. What binds them together and gives them a sense of purpose has been brought to life by a discourse of diversity and the benefits to be derived from such a social and political arrangement. Canada may not be perfect, but it could be a beacon for other countries negotiating the rapids that globalization and hyper-mobility have stirred up on this planet. Our next task is to explore whether Albertans buy into this new narrative.

# 8

## The Alberta Story

By this point the reader will have some understanding of the ways in which Canadian values have been shaped. The chapter on how opinions are formed illustrates how Albertans have been influenced by politicians, the media and other influential groups. However, I would suggest that there is something else at work beyond merely influencing how citizens form their opinions in the short-term. It could be argued that for over half a century a new Alberta identity has been under construction. The Manning government began the differentiation process in 1944, although the soil had already been tilled. The Lougheed government continued on this path when it engaged in province-building, and the process has proceeded seamlessly to the present day.

The previous chapter dealt with ways in which identities (which can be national or regional) can be fashioned by mining the past or by painting an optimistic picture of the future. The importance of language in this project cannot be exaggerated. Ernest Gellner remarked: "Nationalism is not the awakening of nations to self-consciousness: it invents nations where they do not exist" (1983: 69). As language is the raw material that accomplishes the task, some scholars turn their attention to the discourse that is prevalent in a particular society. In its ordinary sense, discourse is a conversation, but in this usage it refers to a specialized vocabulary and set of statements used to discuss and frame a topic in a certain way. National identities are thus brought to life through discourses that draw boundaries between communities. Sub-national identities can be constructed in the same way.

The material about political discourse focuses on language and narratives to show how words can be deployed to achieve political goals. As weapons, words can be more effective than missiles and they are the weapons of a democratic society, used by politicians to good effect. Pointing out that politicians are "professional narrators" Poggo argues that:

> [T]heir accounts display awareness of the poetic power of their words: they know that their success depends on their ability to tell good stories, to find evocative images, to produce seductive metaphors, to convey the right degree of pathos (2002: 327).

Words can rouse passions and soothe them. They can bind people together or split them apart. Deployed in the service of creating an identity, language is exclusionary, marking off one community from others, creating an "Us" and a "Them," or an "Other."

## Constructing "Us" in Alberta

Manning began to construct a new image when he reoriented his party in the course of his first election as Socred leader. As we have seen, constructing an identity is a political exercise with a political purpose that politicians and other interested parties nurture and sustain. Manning's initial goal was short-term: to prevent Social Credit's strongest rival, the CCF, from gaining a foothold in the province. However, he did continue to foster and sustain the negative image of the CCF and the socialist values that underpinned it. Consequently, what began as an election tactic turned into an enduring element in provincial discourse.

Alberta needed to be redefined for two reasons: first, Social Credit had to find a new *raison d'être*, as it was unsuccessful in implementing key legislation, and second, because the identity of interests on the Prairies was dissolving. In addition, Alberta's sister province, Saskatchewan, had just elected a CCF government. The Premier saw a need to present a clear alternative to the siren call of socialism, and thus the first thread was woven into the new identity: Alberta was reinvented as a friend of free enterprise, having repented its flirtation with socialist policies in Social Credit's first administration.[1]

The first task was to rally the population behind a new provincial narrative, one that would inevitably construct internal divisions. The positive image in Manning's Alberta was exemplified by those who rejected the dependency that socialism was believed to breed. These new Albertans had shaken off the Depression mentality, were optimistic, self-reliant and proud of their ability to handle life's challenges.

Despite the anti-socialist discourse, as we have seen, the government was very generous in its funding for education and social programs. However, Finkel rightly points out that, although the Alberta government spent more per capita than any other government in Canada, this was an artifact of "rich" government rather than "big" government: that is, a government that was more left-leaning (1989: 139). Whether the government was right- or left-leaning depends on what one focused on. Manning used a right-wing vocabulary to broaden his party's support, but if the social democrats judged him by his policies they would reach a different conclusion. Thus, everyone was happy.

After the Social Credit defeat, Peter Lougheed's government, in concert with provincial elites, was preoccupied with province-building. Allan Tupper points out that one aspect of the exercise is forging a provincial identity that binds citizens to their province and generates loyalties that are sometimes in conflict with national attachments. The Premier is described by Tupper as "Alberta's most determined, most innovative and successful province-builder" who developed a new sense among Albertans about their distinctive role in Canada and the status of the provincial political community (2004: 204).

That Albertans absorbed the message is evident from the western separatist movement in the 1980s. When the province was locked in battle with the federal government during the energy crisis, two separatist parties, West-Fed and the Western Canada Concept, were active in the province. Shortly after the 1980 National Energy Program was unveiled, their rallies attracted thousands of people. McKinsey points out that not everyone who attended the rallies was a separatist, but polls

---

1. There is some inconsistency in Aberhart's views of socialism, probably reflecting Douglas's contradictory and shifting opinions of the "enemy."

at the time showed support for separatism spiking at 23% (1981:213). The relevance of the separatists to this discussion is the way they tapped into the perceived anti-socialist, self-reliant image of Albertans. In a classic demonstration of "othering," their appeal was: "Join us if you are revulsed [i.e., feel revulsion] at the thought of [take your pick] a centralist, socialist, elitist, dictatorial republic of Central Canada" (cited in McKinsey, 1981:215). In this instance the objective was to create a sense of belonging in the province and to invite Albertans to take the next logical step and separate, presumably with the other western provinces, from the national community.

The construction of Alberta's identity rested on the claim that, unlike others, Albertans had no time for so-called socialist policies and practices. However, the disparity between words and actions, first demonstrated by Manning, continued and has become an enduring feature in the Alberta story. In a 1979 article, just prior to the introduction of the NEP, Gibbins described the attitudes of Albertans this way:

> A strong belief in the spirit if not necessarily the practice of free enterprise, a concomitant belief in the desirability if not the actuality of small, fiscally conservative governments, a tolerance of if not affection for one-party government, and an intense commitment to provincial control of energy resources are all readily acknowledged components of the Alberta political culture (1979: 143).

He was referring to the fact that Albertans were comfortable with the Lougheed government's interventionist policies while supporting free enterprise in principle.

With regard to the Klein government, Nikiforuk's (2002) article, mentioned in Chapter 5, points out numerous differences between the rhetoric and the actions which led him to question Klein's carefully cultivated image as a right-wing economic hero.

The Alberta story of "Us" is that of an enterprising province with a small government and a population that is self-reliant and innovative. As these qualities are often associated with Americans, it is not surprising that many people draw parallels between Albertans and their southern neighbours. The self-portrait flatters and obscures the true picture while driving a wedge between Albertans and other Canadians, particularly in Central Canada. Since the 1940s, one strand in the narrative has been that the province is a desert for left-wing (as defined by the government of the day) ideas. This message has been hammered home repeatedly, the left has been dismissed as irrelevant even as the governing party has introduced measures that would gladden the heart of an NDP Premier.

Another element in the provincial story is that Albertans sweep a party off the political map and turn to something never tried before. The anti-socialist rhetoric takes care of the NDP; the UFA and Social Credit are not longer contenders, so this leaves the Liberals as the only other party that has held office in the province. Over the years, the Conservatives have discredited them by linking them with their unpopular federal cousins and arguing that Albertans will never elect a Liberal government. This is a convenient strategy designed to marginalize their main political opponent.

## Ottawa as the Other

The importance of the role of "othering" in constructing an identity is emphasized by a number of scholars. Some trace "othering" back to the Old Testament, which contains narratives on forging the Hebrew identity and distinguishing it from the Other. In more recent history, during the Cold War the two super-powers cast their opponent as the Other. As the goal is to foster a shared sense of belonging in a community, inevitably there will be a binary opposite and Alberta has one.

In the absence of cultural or other forms of glue, sharing a geographic space (which then becomes a political space) may be the starting point in the attempt to distinguish the target group from the Other. Some would argue that the Canadian Other is the United States, and Alberta's Other is primarily Ottawa, which is seen as a surrogate for Central Canada. The casting of Ottawa as the Other was not a very difficult task, as the prairie provinces had long felt victimized by federal policies that discriminated against the region. The ground was fertile as people right across the Prairies shared the belief that they were a virtual colony of Central Canada. When Aberhart was in power, battling the federal government with his government's provocative legislation, Albertans began to develop a sense that the province was singled out for political humiliation. Thus antagonism towards the federal government was almost bred in the bone.

Although previous Alberta governments had reason to distrust Ottawa, Aberhart's government had an extremely acrimonious relationship with its federal counterpart. Abortive legislation passed by the Social Credit government only served to make the Premier more popular. He benefitted from every invalidation of his government's controversial legislation, as he could then point to Ottawa and the financial institutions that were the target of the legislation as "the true enemies of the will of the people of Alberta" (Caldarola, 1979: 42). His hostility towards the federal government did not end there, and subsequent events solidified it.

There is also evidence that poor advice from Douglas and his representatives in Alberta aggravated (perhaps caused?) the problem. I have already alluded to the fact that Aberhart was completely out of his depth when he became Premier. He had no political experience, did not understand how the political system worked and was desperate for advice. This was not the first time in Alberta or in other provinces that a government was so ill-prepared to exercise power. Arguably the UFA was in a similar position. The difference is that the UFA had a Brownlee in its ranks, someone who understood the imperatives of parliamentary government as well as its constraints. Aberhart had a potential Brownlee in his caucus, Attorney General John Hugill, and he could have depended on him for advice. However, Aberhart's ear was tuned to Douglas and his representatives in Alberta, and Hugill's story demonstrates this quite conclusively.

Hugill was a lawyer and one-time secretary to then-Prime Minister R.B. Bennett. His stint in Aberhart's Cabinet was shortlived; he was forced to resign in 1937. His resignation was the culmination of dramatic events involving John Hargrave, leader of the Green Shirts (uniformed Social Crediters in Britain), who manipulated Aberhart. Hargrave, a rather dubious character,[2] drafted an unsolicited plan to implement Social Credit which Aberhart was obliged to allow him to present to caucus. After the presentation Hugill pointed out that the

---

2. The Green Shirts participated in drilling as well as "Study, Propaganda and Demonstration." Hargrave had previously organized a semi-occult movement dedicated to outdoor life, which was called the "Kindred of the Kibbo Kift." The manual it used was borrowed by the Nazi youth movement (Elliott and Moore, 1987: 186).

SOURCE: GLENBOW ARCHIVES M-1753-3

*"The Attorney-General's Dilemma." One of a series of anti-Social Credit and anti-William Aberhart cartoons drawn by Stewart Cameron, political cartoonist for the Calgary Herald newspaper (January 20, 1940).*

proposed measures would be unconstitutional; he was shouted down and laughed at (Elliott and Miller, 1987: 252–53). His advice was disregarded.

The end came in August 1937, when Lieutenant-Governor John Bowen asked Hugill his opinion on three Bills to which Bowen had been asked to give Royal Assent. (Both Hugill and Aberhart had been summoned to Bowen's office.) The Attorney-General answered that, in his opinion, the Bills were unconstitutional, but Aberhart insisted that the Lieutenant-Governor sign them and said that he would take full responsibility for them. Aberhart asked for Hugill's resignation immediately and took over the Attorney General's portfolio himself (Elliott and Moore, 1987: 267–68). Had the Premier heeded the advice of his Attorney General instead of that of Douglas's advisers, he might have been more successful with the legislation he wished to pass.

The three Bills in question were clearly outside provincial jurisdiction and Mackenzie King suggested a reference to the Supreme Court on the proposed legislation. Aberhart refused and the Bills were disallowed by the federal government, to the delight of Major Douglas. He wired his appointees George Powell and Denis Byrne: "Magnificent... Give Mounties notice. Organize provincial police. Ultimate success now certain..." (Hesketh, 1997: 164–65). Douglas was confident that "Finance" (this was shorthand for banks, financial institutions and the shadowy figures that controlled them) would be unmasked and Albertans would understand the conspiracy to thwart Social Credit. Hesketh points out that

> Douglas's strategy depended on an awakened, directed public will. Try as he might, like Aberhart, Douglas would be unable to mobilize the public behind his strategy. Enthusiasm for his confrontational tactics waned as the grass-roots membership of Social Credit had little taste for his war rhetoric (1987: 165).

Here we have evidence that the actions counseled by Douglas and supported by Aberhart were not at the behest of members of the Social Credit League (it did not style itself as a political party), much less the citizens of Alberta. That Douglas had an agenda is revealed in his reaction to disallowance of the Bills: he wanted to provoke a reaction not only from Ottawa (by firing the Mounties), but also from an aroused population. Albertans did not take the bait but Aberhart continued to heed his advice.

The Depression had almost bankrupted some provinces, so Mackenzie King's government established a Royal Commission on Dominion-Provincial Relations (also referred to as the Rowell-Sirois Commission) in 1937. Hesketh argues that Major Douglas opposed the Commission, as he rejected anything the federal government proposed. His rationale was that it was a ploy to centralize power in Ottawa under the control of Finance. Aberhart had intended to participate in the hearings, although he registered his complaints about the composition of the Commission, but Douglas's opposition made him change his mind. Instead, the Alberta government's submission entitled *The Case for Alberta*, was presented to the "Sovereign People of Canada" (Hesketh, 1997: 180–81).

The publication provided an opportunity for the Alberta government to criticize Ottawa for centralization and to catalogue the region's woes. Douglas's fingerprints are all over this document, as the guidelines for preparing it were drafted by George Powell, one of his emissaries.

The Rowell-Sirois Commission presented its report in 1940 and it was promptly condemned by Aberhart. Douglasites felt it advocated a concentration of power in the federal government which, predictably, they saw "as part of an international financial plot against provincial autonomy" (Elliott and Moore, 1987: 297). Social Credit's opposition to centralization did not come from the grassroots, nor did it emanate from the government. It flowed directly from Douglas's obsession with the perceived threat posed by Finance. Alberta's strong opposition to centralization continued, even intensified, long after Social Credit was defeated.

The word "centralization" has become one of those condensation symbols that is evoked to trigger emotions and memories so the audience will react in a predictable manner. Even though centralization was decoupled from the fear of Finance, suspicion of federal motives took root and another thread was woven into the Alberta identity. As a consequence, any initiative proposed by Ottawa was (and still is) viewed with suspicion by the province, and often rejected.

Ernest Manning, although much more restrained and dignified than his mentor, was no less suspicious of the federal government. We have seen in Chapter 2 that he prevented any federal interference in the province's natural gas industry by setting up a single gas gathering system within the province. His government also battled Ottawa over medicare and other social programs that were being put in place after World War II.

One could argue that Manning's opposition to health care was likewise grounded in the fear of centralization, although some argue that his religion was also a factor. Finkel points out that, like other fundamentalists, Manning believed that humans are essentially alone in their struggle for salvation. Thus, "a collectivist state belittled this struggle and made individuals more vulnerable to behaviour that might lead to eternal damnation": (1989: 136). He was especially opposed to "state collectivism" i.e. universally provided social programs. However, Watkins points to the contradictions and inconsistencies in Manning's core beliefs. He quotes from a speech Manning made shortly after he assumed office, in which he said:

> Every Canadian should have access to all essential medical services and educational facilities. A healthy and well-informed people is essential to a vigorous democracy, and moreover, access to proper health and educational services in this modern age *should be the right of a free and sovereign people* [emphasis mine] (1980: 147).

I would venture to suggest that the major reason for the Manning government's resistance to universal programs like medicare was the source—i.e., because they were proposed by the federal government. Like Douglas, the Premier continued to believe in the conspiracy theories about socialists and Communists controlling the world, so his opposition to what he regarded as centralization of power in Canada was fear of the conspirators.

When the Progressive Conservatives came to office, Alberta society had changed dramatically. However, the conjunction of the energy crisis and constitutional negotiations pitted Premier Lougheed against a federal government that seemed intent on depriving Albertans of their birthright. He vowed that he would "never be part of any form of capitulation to Ottawa on the resource question" (Hustak, 1979:173). During the decade-long battle with Ottawa, and to a lesser extent Ontario, ancient grievances and humiliating experiences were revived and the "Othering" process continued. The argument that resonated most was that now that the province had finally achieved enviable prosperity from a resource that had to be fought for, neither the federal government nor Ontario could tolerate it. The external threat was a very effective instrument in ensuring provincial unity. It is one the Klein government uses frequently in its battles with Ottawa.

Over time, Albertans have been conditioned to view federal initiatives with suspicion to ensure they support decentralization. However, there is evidence that Alberta governments are not opposed to centralization per se, as it flourishes at the provincial level. Critics of Aberhart's government accused the Premier of hypocrisy in fighting centralization in Ottawa when he had stripped responsibilities from local authorities and centralized all provincial power in Edmonton. This charge has been leveled at the Klein government as observers watched the accretion of power in the provincial capital and specifically in the Premier's office. Political scientist Keith Brownsey argues that the concentration of power in the Premier's office began soon after Ralph Klein took over the reins of the party. Cabinet committees were abandoned, bureaucratic agencies were dismantled and these moves enabled Klein to control all aspects of government (2005: 27).

For decades the strategy of Alberta governments has been to seize opportunities to accuse the federal government of ignoring Alberta's interests or the wishes of Albertans. In such cases it was assumed that the government expressed the Voice of Alberta. Senate reform is an issue on which the Klein government has taken Ottawa to task and it provides the clearest recent evidence of the dissonance between the Alberta government's priorities and those of its population.

Most Canadians favour Senate reform, as do most Albertans; however, it is not at the top of the public agenda. Reform of the Senate has been championed in Alberta since the 1980s, and in 1985 the provincial government charged a Special Select Committee with the job of investigating ways to reform the upper house. In 1987, the Alberta legislature endorsed the Committee's report, thus giving its blessing to what is now referred to as the "Triple-E" senate: i.e., one that is equal, elected and effective. That same year, Alberta held a senatorial election as a result of which Stan Waters from the Reform Party was elected.[3] Waters was subsequently appointed by the Mulroney government, as it needed Alberta's support for the Meech Lake Accord.

Since then the province has held two more elections, but the winners have not been appointed by the Prime Minister. The provincial narrative is that the federal government is ignoring the democratically expressed wishes of Alberta voters and that this is a slap in the face of the citizens of Alberta. The other strand in the narrative is that Senate reform is a high priority for Albertans. Even a cursory look at this matter shows that these claims are questionable.

In 1998 Albertans had their second opportunity to vote for

---

3. The legislation authorizing the election is called the "Senatorial Selection Act."

Doreen Barrie

"senators-in-waiting" when an election was held in conjunction with municipal elections across the province. The Klein Conservatives called the election, but no Conservative candidates were nominated to run for these positions. The election was boycotted by both the Liberals and the New Democrats, so two individuals from the Reform Party and two Independents who failed to get the Reform nomination were the only names on the ballot. Turnout was low, as it usually is in municipal elections, and indicates how lukewarm voters were to electing senators.

The third Senate election was held in conjunction with the provincial election in November 2004. The Premier belatedly agreed to let Senate candidates run under the Progressive Conservative banner only because there was pressure from his caucus. Neither the Liberals nor the New Democrats ran candidates in the election, and the Conservative commitment appeared half-hearted: the Party did not provide support to candidates, nor did it do anything to promote the Senate election which was overshadowed by the provincial race.

Turnout in the 2004 provincial election was 44%, a historic low, and of that number over 20% declined, rejected or spoiled their ballots for the Senate vote. Interestingly, the Chief Electoral Officer (CEO) reported that 2.1 million votes were cast for Senatorial candidates. This figure is considerably higher than the number of valid votes cast in the election, which, according to the Elections Alberta website, was 714,709.[4] The figure quoted by the CEO implies that the vote was well supported, but it was arrived at by counting each "X" marked on the Senate ballot. Because each voter could choose up to four senatorial candidates there were over two million Senate votes.

The Klein government dispatched the senators-elect on a cross-country trip in the spring of 2005 to promote Senate reform. Journalist Paul Stanway (2005) speculates that Ralph Klein probably hoped that Air Canada might lose the group "somewhere over northern Ontario and that [it] would be the last we'd hear on a subject that is not exactly at the top of his 'to do' list." Klein did not accede to their request to present the case for Senate reform to the Premiers at the Council of the Federation meeting in Banff in August 2005.

---

4. The Alberta Elections website also notes that the total number of names on the List of Electors for the provincial election was 2,001,287.

– 124 –

Despite evidence that even those Albertans who support Senate reform were not in favour of the election, the Premier, whose own actions show that he is less than enthusiastic, has sharply criticized the federal government for not appointing any of the winners. He has suggested that such insults to Albertans only fuel western alienation.

Lisac points to other examples of the gap between the views and wishes of the population and those of the provincial government: there is overwhelming (79%) support for the National Health Council which the Alberta government refused to join, and 60% of Albertans favour public automobile insurance which the government has also rejected (2004: 27).

The fight for provincial rights, province-building and decentralization are all priorities of the Alberta government, so the assumption has been that the Alberta population, being different from citizens elsewhere, either demanded these policies or support them strongly. They have been accepted as features of the Alberta political culture and are taken as given. Taking a closer look at these assumptions, like the assumption about Senate elections, tells a very different story.

Let us first look at provincial rights. In 1905 when Alberta became a province, there is no question that it, like Saskatchewan and Manitoba, it was treated in a discriminatory fashion. Consequently, succeeding provincial governments fought to secure rights to land and natural resources, as well as an end to policies that were detrimental to the region. Thus, one could argue that provincial rights have been important in the province almost since its inception. However, at that time prairie governments were lobbying for the federal government to do more for the region rather than to leave it alone. The problems—transportation policies, the tariff and natural resource ownership—required federal action.

At that time, provincial rights did not mean pushing away from the rest of the country and erecting a firewall[5] around the province. It was

5. In an open letter to the Premier in January 2001 six prominent Albertans (including Stephen Harper), recommended that Ralph Klein adopt the Alberta Agenda (subsequently dubbed the "firewall") to assert provincial autonomy. Their advice was that the province set up its own pension plan and its own police force to replace the RCMP. It should also collect its own income tax, challenge the Canada Health Act and get Senate reform back on the national agenda.

*Regional differences—and alienation—are not restricted to Quebec, as demonstrated in this political cartoon of Ralph Klein.*

the Social Credit government which began the now-familiar antagonistic relationship with Ottawa, and it is now a permanent feature of the Alberta government's strategy.

The Alberta narrative in the 21st century is still wrapped around western alienation. Although grievances that the province had in its first few decades have been addressed, and despite the fact that provincial coffers are overflowing, the siege mentality is still fostered. Political elites invoke Western alienation to mobilize the troops, and "carriers of the creed" (see Chapter 5) either benefit from fanning the flames or make a career of perpetuating the phenomenon. From the perspective of Canadians in other provinces, Alberta's defensive attitude is hard to fathom and within the province it is becoming increasingly hard to sustain.

The almost unassailable status of Western alienation has been questioned by political scientist Robert Lawson in an article in the *Journal of Canadian Studies*. He argues that western alienation is experienced by some political elites in Alberta but that "this kind of alienation does not account for the disaffection and discontent of many citizens in the

West" (2005: 130). He contends that what is labeled as western alienation is experienced on the eastern periphery as well, suggesting that it is a regional phenomenon which one researcher, Shawn Henry, has labeled "Peripheral Regional Alienation" (cited in Lawson, 2005: 135). However, Lawson also points out that data from the Canada Election Surveys, which are conducted nationally, show a level of political alienation (i.e., estrangement from political representatives and the system) right across the country including in Ontario (2005: 141). Alienation may be a much wider phenomenon as citizens in many provinces, and indeed many democracies, grow disillusioned about the political process.

Another point that Lawson makes is that regional alienation is pervasive *within* the western region. He points to a study conducted by Philip Resnick who found that residents in remote regions of B.C. felt they were ignored by Victoria and the Lower Mainland, and that their discontent is analogous to alienation of the West from the federal government (2005: 134–35).

Although I am not aware that a similar study has been conducted in Alberta, there is some evidence of intra-provincial dissatisfaction. Bob Clark who chaired the 2002–03 Alberta Electoral Boundaries Commission, presented his findings at a seminar in the Political Science Department at the University of Calgary in 2003. In his presentation he commented that, during the course of public hearings in northern Alberta, residents complained about being ignored by Edmonton and generally marginalized. Their feelings were similar to those uncovered by Resnick in his study, a sense that less-populated areas counted for little. What was most intriguing was his statement that some rural Albertans suggested that, given their declining electoral weight, it might be a good idea to have an upper house at the provincial level to represent the interests of sparsely populated areas.

Lawson also challenges proponents of western alienation who "attempt to generalize across the West on the basis of data and experiences taken largely from Alberta" (2005: 135–36). He contends that

> [j]ust because the discourse about alienation in western Canada has been successfully captured and subsequently framed by adherents to the western alienation thesis does not render it the most appropriate explanation of the problem of alienation in western Canada (2005: 148–49).

The Alberta identity has been under a construction for decades, woven around values like self-reliance and governments that support free enterprise. Other threads include western alienation, decentralization and antagonism towards the federal government. It has been constructed mainly in the language of resentment and discontent. We have seen how the individual strands came into existence and how they were fabricated and woven into the tapestry. While no one denies that previous generations had to fight to secure provincial rights and that the region was set up as a colony for Central Canada, that time has long passed.

The province of Alberta has traveled a long way during the century since its birth. In the process, Albertans have honed many skills, experienced joy and sorrow. During the last hundred years, despite trials and tribulations, they have remained optimistic about the future. This is why it is so baffling that ancient grievances continue to be nourished. Perhaps turning 100 is a good time to construct a different story, one that is more positive, less angry and less resentful. It is time to put down the violins and pick up trumpets instead, to emphasize the positive qualities Albertans possess and focus on the contributions this province has made to the country. An essential element in the new provincial narrative must surely be that Albertans share fundamental Canadian values, feel kinship with people in other parts of Canada and are eager to play a larger role on the national stage. There are many attractive aspects to this province and a brand new story waiting to be told.

# 9

## Conclusion

It is most unfortunate that Alberta is considered so politically boring, so socially predictable and economically smug. At least we have a past!

The province's first three decades were turbulent, challenging and also exciting when Albertans, along with other prairie residents, fought hard against the elements, discriminatory treatment and unjust policies. The early grievances seem to be permanently etched only on the collective memory of Albertans. Dissatisfaction persists in Alberta despite vast wealth and this is mystifying. Perhaps readers will be less baffled now that they understand how skillfully the sense of grievance has been fostered by provincial elites.[1]

Albertans abandoned the political mainstream for half a century, experimenting with new political parties (which insisted they were not parties!), strange monetary theories and some fairly radical ideas. This was enough to raise a few eyebrows in the rest of the country. Alberta has since constructed a new identity for itself, one that is modern,

---

1. I must point out that Albertans are understandably concerned about moves that might threaten their petroleum resources. No other natural resource attracts so much federal attention. Because oil and gas are depleting resources, the province needs to maximize the benefits derived from them. That Albertans are more generous than many believe is evident from a recent poll (Donolo and Gregg, 2005).

dynamic and "world class." Contemporary, air-brushed Alberta provides a very distorted picture of the province, stripping it of its lively history and the ferment of those early years.

The new identity has no room for the different strands in the ideological tapestry that existed until the early 1940s. The new story about the province was constructed with a set of carefully selected and very familiar building blocks. These drew on non-partisan tendencies, exploitation of the region by the Centre and an appeal to distinguishing characteristics which are deemed to set Alberta apart.

Identities can be "magicked" into existence for political purposes: to mobilize, to call for sacrifices or cement social solidarity. The political purpose served by the Alberta identity was to produce a reliable reserve army of Albertans for the numerous skirmishes with Ottawa. A useful by-product was marginalization of opposition parties and reinforcement of non-partisanship.

Non-partisanship is the most enduring characteristic in Alberta's political culture, smoothing the path for governments and throwing up roadblocks for opposition parties. One consequence of nonpartisanship has been an aversion to and suspicion of the cut and thrust of political debate. Politics itself is almost a four-letter word, denoting an unsavoury activity not even elected officials will admit they engage in. The view that politics is grubby and divisive echoes through the province's history, giving Alberta a surreal, apolitical feel.

While it is laudable to seek compromise and avoid controversy, what political leaders in Alberta have succeeded in doing is to convince the population that governing is just managing and presiding over a large administrative apparatus. The nonpartisan discourse obscures political choices which are made on a daily basis, choices which confer benefits on some and costs on others.

A more serious consequence is that because Albertans have been weaned on consensus, there is a tendency to frown on dissent itself, to consider opposition disloyal. Alberta has rarely had numerically strong opposition, so the practical benefits of vigourous political debate have yet to be experienced.

The Alberta Story tells a flattering tale about a population that is proud, self-reliant and individualistic, and a government that caters to these qualities. The great disparity between the discourse and the reality is overlooked because the province's affluence has not required the people to exercise these independent characteristics. Nor have Albertans noticed that provincial governments have not been mere night watchmen standing on the sidelines of the economy and society. Governments in Alberta have demonstrated remarkable flexibility and pragmatism as have governments elsewhere.

To argue that Albertans resemble Canadians in other parts of the country will be resisted by those who buy into and seek to perpetuate the Alberta Story. It would not work if the population felt kinship with the Other. Nevertheless, it should be apparent by now that the differences between "us" and "them" are overstated. More important is an understanding of *why* they are overstated, why there has been a campaign to construct a distinctive Alberta identity.

The strategies and techniques that are used to construct identities over the long term, and opinions in the short-term, are applicable in every democracy. As human beings we are open to flattery, persuasion and coercion. Despite drowning in a sea of information, many citizens continue to take their cues from prominent people or form their opinions based on media coverage that is often superficial and biased. Understanding the techniques that are used and the weapons that can be deployed will at least enable people to be aware of the potential for manipulation.

Governments nowadays have a modern arsenal not only to shape public opinion but to create it. In Alberta the task is vastly simplified as there is little competition for the allegiance of the population. There are pockets of resistance to the dominant narrative, but they are scattered and too weak to dislodge it. The narrative is supported by the government and powerful groups that have the resources to nurture it. Thus, even the most dedicated opponents throw up their hands in despair.

The population is susceptible to the suggestion that Alberta's treasury is going to be raided and, once again, there is talk of separation. While not separatists, supporters of the firewall solution whose slogan is "More Alberta, Less Ottawa" are keen to detach the province from the federal government. They would favour a sort of sovereignty-association for the province, and in their quest for it they attempt to rekindle the incandescent outrage Albertans felt when the NEP was introduced.

What they fail to recognize is that Albertans have grand ambitions and a burning desire to play a lead role on the national stage. They want to be noticed, respected and acknowledged as being an important part of Canada. If they had to adopt a slogan, it would be: "More Alberta in Ottawa." Instead they are seen as the cry-babies of Confederation and selfish to boot.

Canada is a difficult country to govern because of its vast size and its scattered and diverse population. The task is doubly difficult when practically everything the national government wants to do is challenged by the Premiers. The construction of a national or provincial narrative is not a trivial matter. Constructing an Other is a political act and could have serious political consequences.

This book challenges a number of assumptions and cherished beliefs in this province but in 21st-century Alberta they need to be scrutinized more critically. My hope is that readers will approach the analysis with an open mind and conduct a reality check when provincial elites purport to speak on their behalf. It is not easy to challenge the dominant narrative because it is so deeply entrenched, but it is worth a try!

At the time of writing there is an ongoing debate about how the provincial government should spend the vast surpluses generated by rapid increases in oil and gas prices. The Klein government is being accused of being short-sighted and lacking in a vision for the future. When the road ahead is being mapped out, it may also be time to construct a more uplifting, more textured narrative for this province, one that is inclusive, that emphasizes that Albertans feel part of a national community and are eager to work to strengthen it.

The Other Story of Alberta can be written by selecting different ingredients from the same reservoir as the official story. At the very least it would acknowledge the gaps and silences in the official narrative. It would also consign ancient grievances to the archives and focus on the positive contributions the province has made to Confederation. It would not speak in the language of resentment and alienation. All that is required is imagination, creativity and empathy, qualities that Albertans have in abundance.

For the new Alberta narrative to take root, people in other provinces will have to shed the "Ugly Albertan" image and Albertans will have to adopt a more positive view of Ottawa and Central Canada. Now who will cast the first kiss?

# Bibliography

Allen, Richard. 1985. "Social Gospel as the Religion of the Agrarian Revolt." Pp. 439–49 in R. Douglas Francis and Howard Palmer (eds.), *The Prairie West: Historical Readings*. Edmonton: University of Alberta Press.

Anderssen, Erin, Michael Valpy, et al. 2004. *The New Canada: A Globe and Mail Report on the Next Generation*. Toronto: A Globe and Mail/McClelland Stewart Book.

Anderson, Benedict. 1983. *Imagined Communities: Reflections on the Origin and Spread of Nationalism*. London: Verso.

Anderson, Walter Truett. 1990. *Reality Isn't What It Used To Be*. San Francisco: Harper San Francisco, A Division of Harper Collins.

Barr, John. 1974. *The Dynasty: The Rise and Fall of Social Credit in Alberta*. Toronto: McLelland and Stewart Limited.

Barrie, Doreen. 1980. "Canadian Political Culture: Integration and Fragmentation" (Master's thesis, University of Calgary).

Bell, David. 1994. *Social Classes and Social Credit in Alberta*. Montreal: McGill-Queen's University Press.

Bell, David and Lorne Tepperman. 1970. *The Roots of Disunity: Political Culture in Canada*. Toronto: McCelland and Stewart.

Bennett, W. Lance. 1988. *News: The Politics of Illusion*. New York: Longman.

Black, Edwin R. 1982. *Politics and the News: The Political Functions of the Mass Media*. Toronto: Butterworths.

Brownsey, Keith. 2005. "Ralph Klein and the Hollowing of Alberta." Pp. 23–36 in Trevor Harrison (ed.), *The Return of the Trojan Horse: Alberta and the New World (Dis)Order*. Montreal: Black Rose Books.

Brzozowska, Anna. 2003. "Symbols, Myths and Metaphors: The Discursive Battle Over the True Belarusian Narrative," *Slova* 15, no. 1 (Spring): 49–58.

Byford, Jovan. 2004. "From 'Traitor' to 'Saint' in Public Memory: The Case of Serbian Bishop Nikolaj Velimirovic," *Analysis of Current Trends in Antisemitism (ACTA)* 23. Jerusalem: Sassoon International Centre for the Study of Antisemitism, Hebrew University.

Cairns, Alan C. 1977. "The Governments and Societies of Canadian Federalism," *Canadian Journal of Political Science* 10, no. 4 (December): 696–725.

Caldarola, Carlo. 1979. *Society and Politics in Alberta: Research Papers.* Toronto: Methuen.

Conrad, Margaret. 2001. "Historical Consciousness, Regional Identity and Public Policy." Paper presented at Canadian Historical Consciousness in an International Context: Theoretical Frameworks, University of British Columbia, Vancouver, BC.

Curran, James. 1991. "Mass Media and Democracy: A Reappraisal." Pp. 82–117 in James Curran and Michael Gurevitch (eds.), *Mass Media and Society.* London: E. Arnold, A Division of Hodder & Stoughton.

Dacks, Gurston. 1986. "From Consensus to Competition: Social Democracy and Political Culture in Alberta." Pp. 186–204 in Larry Pratt (ed.), *Social Democracy in Alberta: Essays in Honour of Grant Notley.* Edmonton: NeWest Press.

Denis, Claude. 1995. "The New Normal: Capitalist Discipline in Alberta in the 1990s." Pp. 86–100 in Trevor Harrison and Gordon Laxer (eds.), *The Trojan Horse: Alberta and the Future of Canada.* Black Rose Books Ltd.

Donolo, Peter and Allan Gregg. 2005. "What Regional Tensions?" *Globe and Mail* (September 21).

Dyck, Rand. 2000. *Canadian Politics: Critical Approaches*, 3rd ed. Scarborough, ON: Nelson Thomson Learning.

Edelman, Murray. 1964. *The Symbolic Uses of Politics.* Urbana: University of Illinois Press.

Elder, Charles D. and Roger W. Cobb. 1983. *The Political Uses of Symbols.* New York: Longman.

Ellis, Richard J. 2002. *Democratic Delusions: The Initiative Process in America.* Kansas: The University Press of Kansas.

Elliott, David R. and Iris Miller. 1987. *Bible Bill: A Biography of William Aberhart.* Edmonton: Reidmore Books.

Emery, J.C. Herbert and Ronald D. Kneebone. 2005. "Mostly Harmless: Socialists, Populists, Policies and the Economic Development of Alberta and Saskatchewan." Paper prepared for the Institute for Advanced Policy Research, University of Calgary. Technical Paper 05003.

Epp, Roger. 1984. "The Lougheed Government and the Media: News Management in the Alberta Political Environment," *Canadian Journal of Communications* 10, no. 2: 37–65.

———. 2002. "Their Own Schools of Democracy: The Visible Remains of Political Practice in Rural Alberta," Heritage Community Foundation.

http://www.albertasource.ca/aspenland/eng/society/article_schools_democracy.html.

Finkel, Alvin. 1980. *The Social Credit Phenomenon in Alberta*. Toronto: University of Toronto Press.

Friesen, Gerald. 1987. *The Canadian Prairies: A History*. Toronto: University of Toronto Press.

Gellner, Ernest. 1983. *Nations and Nationalism*. Oxford: Blackwell Press.

Gibbins, Roger. 1979. "Western Alienation and Alberta Political Culture." Pp. 143–67 in Carlo Caldarola (ed.), *Society and Politics in Alberta: Research Papers*. Toronto: Methuen.

——. 1980. *Prairie Politics and Society*. Toronto: Butterworths.

Gill, Rosemarie. 1985. "Oil, Policy-making and Power: The Case of Crude Oil Pricing in Canada and Australia, 1973–1981" (Master's thesis, University of Calgary).

Ginsberg, Benjamin. 1986. *The Captive Public: How Mass Opinion Promotes State Power*. New York: Basic Books.

Gwyn, Richard. 1996. *Nationalism Without Walls: The Unbearable Lightness of Being Canadian*. Toronto, Ontario: McClelland & Stewart.

Harrison, Trevor. 2000. "The Changing Face of Prairie Politics: Populism in Alberta," *Prairie Forum* 25, no. 1 (Spring): 107–21.

Hesketh, Bob. 1997. *Major Douglas and Alberta Social Credit*. Toronto: University of Toronto Press.

Hobsbawm, E.J. 1983. *The Invention of Tradition*. Cambridge: Cambridge University Press.

Hofstadter, Richard. n.d. "The Age of Reform. Populism: Nostalgic Agrarianism." http://www.mc.cc.md.us/Departments/hpolscrv/Populism.html.

Horowitz, Gad. 1966. "Conservatism, Liberalism and Socialism in Canada: An Interpretation," *CJEPS* 32, no.2: 143–71.

Hustak, Allan. 1979. *Peter Lougheed: A Biography*. Toronto: McClelland and Stewart.

Ignatieff, Michael. 1993. *Blood and Belonging: Journeys into the New Nationalism*. Toronto: Viking.

Inglehart, Ronald. 2000. "Globalization and Post-Material Values," *The Washington Quarterly* 23, no. 1 (Winter): 215–28.

Kooyman, Susan. 1981. "The Policies and Legislation of the United Farmers of Alberta Government, 1921–1935" (Master's thesis, University of Calgary).

Kuklinski, James H. and Norman Hurley. 1994. "On Hearing and Interpreting Political Messages: A Cautionary Tale of Citizen Cue-Taking," *Journal of Politics* 56, no. 3 (August): 729–51.

Lawson, Robert J. 2005. "Understanding Alienation in Western Canada: Is 'Western Alienation' the Problem? Is Senate Reform the Cure?," *Journal of Canadian Studies* 39, no. 2: 127–55.

Laycock, David. 1990. *Populism and Democratic Thought in the Canadian Prairies, 1910–1945*. Toronto: University of Toronto Press.

Levesque, Stephane. 2005. "Review essay: 'In Search of a Purpose for School History'," *Journal of Curriculum Studies* 37, no. 3: 349–58.

Limerick, Patricia Nelson. 1995. "Turnerians All: The Dream of a Helpful History in an Intelligible World," *American Historical Review* 100 (June): 697–716.

Lipset, S.M. 1970. *Revolution and Counter-Revolution.* New York: Anchor Books.

———. 1990. *Continental Divide: The Values and Institutions of the United States and Canada.* New York: Routledge.

Lisac, Mark. 1995. *The Klein Revolution.* Edmonton: NeWest Press.

———. 2003. "Ignoring Alberta's Anti-War Protestors: http://www.caj.ca/mediamag/spring2003/Media_SPRING03-11-20.pdf

———. 2004. *Alberta Politics Uncovered: Taking Back our Province.* Edmonton: NeWest Press.

Macpherson, C.B. 1962. *Democracy in Alberta,* 2nd ed. Toronto: University of Toronto Press.

Manzer, Ronald. 1974. *Canada: A Socio-Political Report.* Toronto: McGraw-Hill, Ryerson Limited.

Martin, Don. 2002. *King Ralph: The Political Life and Success of Ralph Klein.* Toronto: Key Porter Books.

Masson, Jack and Peter Blaikie. 1979. "Labour Politics in Alberta." Pp. 271–83 in Carlo Caldarola (ed.), *Society and Politics in Alberta: Research Papers.* Toronto: Methuen.

McKinsey, Lauren. 1981. "Watching the Separatists." Pp. 209–28 in Larry Pratt and Garth Stevenson (eds.), *Western Separatism: The Myths, Realities & Dangers.* Edmonton: Hurtig Publishers.

Miller, David et al. 1987. *Blackwell Encyclopaedia of Political Thought.* Oxford: Blackwell.

Nevitte, Neil. 1996. *The Decline of Deference.* Peterborough: Broadview Press.

Nikiforuk, Andrew. 2002. "Mr. Dress-up," *National Post Magazine* (December 1).

Osborne, Brian S. 2002. "Landscapes, Memory, Monuments, and Commemoration: Putting Identity in its Place." Paper Commissioned by the Department of Canadian Heritage for Ethno-cultural, Racial, Religious and Linguistic Divisions and Identity Seminar," Halifax, Nova Scotia (November 1–2), www.metropolis.net.

Pal, Leslie. 1992. "The Political Executive and Political Leadership in Alberta." Pp. 1–29 in Allan Tupper and Roger Gibbins (eds.), *Government and Politics in Alberta.* Edmonton: University of Alberta Press.

Palmer, Howard and Tamara Palmer. 1990. *Alberta: A New History.* Edmonton: Hurtig.

Poggio, Barbara. 2004. "Casting the 'Other': Gender Citizenship in Politicians' Narratives," *Journal of Language & Politics* 3, no. 2: 328–43.

Pratt, Larry. 1981. "Whose Oil is It?" Pp. 155–71 in Larry Pratt and Garth Stevenson (eds.), *Western Separatism: The Myths, Realities & Dangers.* Edmonton: Hurtig Publishers.

Resnick, Philip. 2005. *The European Roots of Canadian Identity.* Peterborough, ON: Broadview Press.

Richards, John and Larry Pratt. 1979. *Prairie Capitalism: Power and Influence in the New West*. Toronto: McClelland and Stewart.

Richardson, G.H. 2001. "A Border Within: The Western Canada Protocol for Social Studies Education and the Politics of National Identity Construction." Brazil: VIII Congreso AMEC.

Rolph, William Kirby. 1950. *Henry Wise Wood of Alberta*. Toronto: University of Toronto Press.

Sampert, Shannon. 2005. "King Ralph, the Ministry of Truth, and the Media in Alberta." Pp. 37–51 in Trevor W. Harrison (ed.), *The Return of the Trojan Horse: Alberta and the New World (Dis)Order*. Montreal: Black Rose Books.

Seixas, Peter. 2000. "History's Fractured Mirror," *Globe and Mail* (December 26).

Simeon, Richard and David Elkins. 1974. "Regional Political Cultures in Canada," *Canadian Journal of Political Science* 7, no. 3 (September).

Stanway, Paul. 2005. "Senate Reform Needs Ralph's Full Support," *Edmonton Sun* (July 29).

Stevenson, Garth. 1985. "Quasi-Democracy in Alberta." Pp. 278–82 in Hugh Thorburn (ed.), *Political Parties in Canada*, 5th ed. Scarborough, ON: Prentice-Hall Canada Inc..

Stinson, Fred. 2002. "American City," *Alberta Views* (March/April): 9–11.

Taras, David. 1990. *The Newsmakers: The Media's Influence on Canadian Politics*. Scarborough, ON: Nelson Canada.

Thayer, Frank. 1998. "Principles and Tactics of Propaganda: Inevitability and Effectiveness of Managing Public Attitudes." Paper presented at the 40th Annual Conference of the Western Social Science Association, 1998.

Thomas, L.G. 1959. *The Liberal Party of Canada: A History of Politics in the Province of Alberta, 1905–21*. Toronto: University of Toronto Press.

Tilson, D.J. 1996. "Promoting a Greener Image of Nuclear Power in the U.S. and Britain," *Public Relations Review* 22, no. 1: 63–79.

Van Loon, Richard J. and Michael S. Whittington. 1987. *The Canadian Political System: Environment, Sturcture and Process*, 4th ed. Toronto: McGraw Hill.

Vivone, Richard (ed.). 2004. *Insight into Government: Alberta's Independent Newsletter on Policy & Politics* 18, no. 30 (April 23).

Watkins, Ernest. 1980. *The Golden Province: Political Alberta*. Calgary: Sandstone Publishing Ltd.

Wilson, John. 1974. "The Canadian Political Cultures: Towards a Re-definition of the Nature of the Canadian Political System," *Canadian Journal of Political Science* 7, no. 3 (September): 438–83.

Wiseman, Nelson. 1995. "The Pattern of Prairie Politics." Pp. 640–60 in *The Prairie West: Historical Readings*, 2nd ed. Edmonton: Pica Pica Press.

Zaller, John R. 1982. *The Nature and Origins of Mass Opinion*. New York: Cambridge University Press.

# Index

Doreen Barrie

6

22     ʃ Alberta (UFA), 7,
25, 29, 56, 62–67,
4, 87, 117–18
ɔf, xi, 20, 29, 64

ael, 38
Richard J., 67
ɛr Sun, 43
Alberta, xiii, 123
κ, Aritha, 2, 6, 19

ʃs, Stan, 123
ɛins, Ernest, 9, 76, 77, 95, 122
lth (of Alberta), vii, 11, 44, 46,
69, 89, 129, 131
estbourne Baptist Church, 49
ʃestern alienation, 55, 70, 126–28,
132
Western Canada Concept, 115
Western Canada Protocol, 106
Western Labour Conference
(Calgary), 72
western separatist movement, 115
West-Fed, 115
wheat economy, 68, 70, 71
wheat pools, 15, 17, 69
White Paper on Human Resources
Development, 21
Whittington, Michael S., 67
Wilson, John, 40
Winnipeg General Strike (1919), 72
Wisconsin, University of, 68
Wiseman, Nelson, 60, 61, 62, 63
women, votes for, 14
Wood, Henry Wise, 10, 14–18,
62–64, 84

Woodsworth, J.S., 49
World War I, xi, 7, 14, 25, 61, 67, 72
World War II, 38, 47, 71, 102, 121

Y
Yellow Pamphlet, 74
Yaffe, Barbara, 43, 60

Z
Zaller, John, 84